The Ferryman's Dream

THE FERRYMAN'S DREAM
AN ORIGINAL LIFE

Dr. Stewart Bitkoff

Abandoned Ladder

ISBN-13: 978-0615613000 (Abandoned Ladder)
ISBN-10: 0615613004

10 9 8 7 6 5 4 3 2 1

In every moment, the Divine Plan is revealed;
Each moment is an opportunity to create- then it is gone.
Living moment by moment, we have the choice to rise higher
Or stay where we are.

O spiritual traveler, consider your moments well.
They are as precious as any treasure you will ever find.
                                    SB

Acknowledgement

Gratitude is extended to Hermann Hesse who first introduced us to the wise ferryman, Vesudeva in the novel <u>Siddhartha</u>. *For those readers who may be unfamiliar with this work, Vesudeva is teacher to Siddhartha, who at the end of his spiritual search works alongside Vesudeva ferrying travelers across the river. In time, this experience completes Siddhartha and helps fulfill his destiny; developing into the Buddha.*

In our present story, Vesudeva again helps ferry travelers across the river, journey inward and discover their own inner potential.

Like merging sources of water into a powerful river, this story uses a traditional technique to weave together different strands and colors. Together this layering of ideas, forms the larger work.

As in life, may this layering help you reach Higher.

*   *

Contents

Introduction: Spiritual University

The duckling was both tired and exhilarated from her struggle. Breaking through the shell had taken hours and as her eyes adjusted to the sunlight, the youngster wondered what to do next. Gazing about, the duckling saw her mother seated nearby observing. With a loving twinkle in her eye, she spoke. "Do not worry. I am here to guide you and I will teach you what you need to know."

∞

For the spiritual traveler, the teacher is the guide who instructs in the next phase of life—spiritual learning. Until this point, breaking free of the shell of patterned thought, everything the traveler needed was inborn and readily available. It was part of biological hardwiring, social learning and conditioning. Now entering a larger world, there are important things to know about and recognize. Because the teacher has traveled this path, learning will be directed, as in the case of the mother duck, by an expert.

∞

The ducklings in the nest are taught everything they need.
They are a completed species.
Humanity is still evolving spiritually;
Although some have reached completion.

These completed souls help others make the journey.
Using tools and faculties termed extraordinary.
Often, the instruction these teachers offer
Is denied or overlooked.

Such is the condition of humanity.

෪

— 1 —

Man's Spiritual Destiny

Man is the meeting point between heaven and earth, and is created with a spiritual destiny. Within man there is the capacity to create, make decisions and destroy. These abilities reflect Higher attributes and man's birth right is to rule a vast, personal spiritual kingdom.

In the journey to unlock one's inner spiritual potential there are many roads, paths and experiences. Learning occurs both on a conscious and unconscious level, often simultaneously. Some lessons are spiritual and others physical, emotional or what is commonly termed mental. Fundamentally, man is a being of conscious energy and must learn to harness this energy or consciousness to reach full capacity.

These learning experiences, in addition to man's inborn potential, develop across many lessons to form the completed person. The completed individual, the end product of striving and development, is a unique being with many individual capacities and abilities that are designed to carry out specific functions.

During their life time, in order for the higher development to be complete, the individual must make both ordinary and higher preparations. Simplistically, the individual must be part of the community within which they find themselves, yet burn for something higher. On one level, the individual must make ordinary adjustments to every day life and be part of the social fabric, yet have within a burning for the Source. A longing to answer life's unanswered questions.

Then according to Plan, a teacher arrives and the individual embraces the missing element. In time and according to design, this interaction alchemizes the soul and consciousness.

Within our universe, there is a primal energy that is life giving, loving and all knowing. This supra-energy or Light is the enabling factor and in time the individual learns to embrace and use this primordial element. Having a part of this element within, slowly the individual recognizes this energy as the Source of their inner burning.

In the journey to completion, each is the prodigal son who returns with spiritual capacity and is embraced by their Father; sharing in the kingdom and their birthright.

ଛ   ଛ

Some Where in Time: Vesudeva awoke, sat at the edge of his bed watching the sunlight play across the window. It was a sunny summer's morn and as he stood and put on his pants, Vesudeva took a slow deep breath inhaling the clean morning air. Smelling the fresh pine and the river's fragrance, he repeated a silent prayer, grateful to be alive.

Five years ago, Vesudeva gave up his life in the city; and moved to this lush river valley; returning to simpler ways. Taking up life as a ferryman, transporting travelers across the great river; he listened to the changing currents and travelers' dreams. In this way, Vesudeva embraced his own inner wisdom. And as he ferried travelers, helping them along their journey, Vesudeva learned to go deep within himself. Inside there was a quiet, restful place. Far from everyday cares, this center was wise, timeless and peaceful. The energy that emanated from this part of his soul was life giving and joyful. Usually, this part came forward in the quiet moments, reaching out, letting Vesudeva understand who he was and how to help others in their travels. Walking along the river shore, Vesudeva watched the morning light sparkle against the rippling water. The light danced through the morning mist, as the mist evaporated upward toward the heavens. Observing this process of changing from liquid, to vapor and ascending, Vesudeva was reminded of the soul's upward journey through the worlds. So many changes: and each change in accord with the great wheel of life.

As the river danced its song of praise and flowed onward, Vesudeva rested on the shore waiting for the first traveler of the day.

ဆာ

It was mid morning and Vesudeva was back at his hut, sipping mint tea prepared over a small fire. Slowly, Vesudeva repeated the prayer. The prayer was an old friend and had become part of him. Often, as he worked and guided the raft full of passengers, Vesudeva recognized another part of his mind was occupied, repeating: *"O Lord, I surrender myself to you."*

In the years he followed this path to completion, Vesudeva came to realize that mind, or what is sometimes called consciousness, has many layers. Ebbing and flowing like the river. Sometimes the patterns were tranquil. Sometimes a storm blew across the surface, but always below the surface there were quiet, peaceful depths that could be traveled.

Even when the river appeared still, it was moving. Like his mind, constantly occupied with thought. In this mental activity there was energy, and the point of spiritual learning was to focus this energy, thereby creating a reality that was both an expression of the Source and an individual expression of self.

ဆာ

Back at work, ready for the next run, Vesudeva bent to inspect the ropes, knots and logs; checking each inch of the raft to make

3

sure it was sound and free of rot. While working on the water, one had to be ever vigilant to protect the passengers. As ferryman, safety was more important than keeping to schedule. Many a crossing was delayed so the raft might be made stronger and fit to travel.

As Vesudeva pushed off and steered upriver, he felt the sun across his brow. The sun was strong and this day promised to grow very warm. Yet as the raft made its way, slowly from the dock and out into the water, there was a breeze at his back. This breeze made the repetitive motion of working the paddle less of a strain and enjoyable. Often, he chose to propel on muscle power and not run the two rear motors. It felt good to move his body in the sun and feel his command of the repetitive, back and forth rowing motion. The life of a ferryman kept him physically fit and provided time alone to journey the deep waters of his soul.

ℕ ℕ

Each person is an individual, unique expression of the Divine.
Having been created with the potential to reach higher
And become more than they are.

All that is required is a conduit. Look closer, it is there.

ℕ

To live in the moment and be free;
To have the courage to be yourself
And create your own life.
That is living a dream.

ℕ

Every one goes through this life
Doing the best they can.
Often travelers are blind to the fact they can reach higher.
The ability to show this to someone is very rare.

— 2 —

What You Believe

Each society and age develops specific ideas, beliefs and goals around which to base their culture. In time, these beliefs become assumptions about life and guiding principles for day to day actions. Rarely are these beliefs or goals questioned and the community is organized formally and informally around them.

In order for the culture to be successful, a majority of people must agree these things are valid and important. Specific beliefs and goals then become both internally and externally accepted. Anyone questioning these is subject to sanctions or pressure from family, friends or themselves. These sanctions could be in the form of punishments from the larger society or simply feelings of personal guilt.

In our culture, we can see examples of these very pervasive beliefs, such as the 'American Dream.' "If you work hard, you can have a good job, home and family, and these things will make you happy."

From the perspective of 'higher consciousness' and living an original life, the traveler must learn to examine assumptions and beliefs. Because of the automatic fashion in which these ideals are incorporated into individual personality; their engineering and false sense of permanence may provide internal stressors that prevent other things from happening.

The spiritual traveler is trying to arrive at a place of balance, where every day thoughts, assumptions and desires are suspended for a time, so something else might happen. This something else is higher knowledge and typically this capacity comes forward only under certain conditions, for example, when the traveler is internally quiet, free of desire or interfering forms of consciousness.

Keep in mind, there is a difference between suspending an idea or belief and trying to obliterate it. We are discussing stilling consciousness, or pushing an idea aside for a limited time. Not pounding on or destroying an idea.

ဢ   ဢ

Seated on the far side of the dock, Nestor waited for the next ferry pickup. Across the river, Nestor could see the ferryman rowing to make the midday run. Usually, this was a busy hour. On this day, people traveled from the city to their suburban homes seeking a quiet, restful interlude in the country. Others, craftsmen and farmers, made this trip two or three times per week to sell their goods in the market.

At this time, besides Nestor there were two other travelers. A young couple dressed for a weekend of camping in the mountains. Nestor had been making this trip for almost four years. It had been that long but the individual days seemed to rush by.

With a smile, Nestor recalled how he had come to the ferryman in a haze of drunken indulgence. It had come about as a dare. A bet made by tavern friends. One night, in the middle of their drinking and smoking games, Nestor and his friends began talking about the ferryman. This talk eventually led to a dare and bet. During the first year that the ferryman had been transporting passengers across the river all kinds of stories and rumors surrounded him. Mysteriously, one day he appeared and replaced the old couple who worked the landing. Nothing had been said. One day, the old couple was gone and without explanation or notice, the ferryman replaced them to work the water route and to live in their old straw hut.

Some said the ferryman was a local man, who had owned a small farm and purchased the ferry business. Others claimed he had been a carpet merchant in the city and a personal tragedy drove him to the country. Still others said he fled from a neighboring province to avoid gambling debts. Yet, others mused he was a mystic who could unlock secrets to an ancient treasure.

Whatever the ferryman's origin, when questioned about himself, usually the ferryman smiled and deflected the inquiry. Sometimes he would turn the question back to the traveler and ask about their life and other times, simply say that he could not answer questions while trying to navigate the dangerous river currents. This air of mystery made some travelers suspicious. Yet, everyone said he was a competent and skilled river man who had a kindly smile and peaceful energy about him.

After more drinks and more tokes on their bong, someone suggested that they all take a trip down to the river, wake up the ferryman and find out exactly who he was. This was intended to be done under the guise of civic spirit; it was not proper that people should put their lives daily in the hands of a man who might be a common criminal.

To make it more interesting, bets were placed on which path led the ferryman to this part of the country. Finally, after much discussion and several more tokes on the bong, it was decided that Nestor travel on behalf of the citizens of Tajjali Tavern to discover the ferryman's origin. Questions needed to be answered. What had he done with the old couple who preceded him and was he a practitioner of black arts?

The sole reason Nestor was selected to go at this late hour, was that he was the only one of the companions who could stand and talk somewhat coherently.

ॐ

As Vesudeva steered across the water, he could see Nestor waiting on the dock. Along side was a young couple who were dressed for their country weekend.

Over the years that Vesudeva had been transporting travelers across the river, he had grown physically stronger and more intuitive. During the long periods, rowing the rear paddle side to side when the outboards were still, Vesudeva moved in tune to the quiet rhythms of river life. Certainly words were useful in understanding and explaining life, its purpose and mystery, but much could be learned by observing and listening with the heart.

Vesudeva came to realize that the quiet rhythms and energy that held all things together could be felt carrying the words that people used to communicate. This energy which supported all things had multiple fluctuations and variations, yet it was singular, life giving and loving. Over many years, Vesudeva realized this energy was the Source: the mother and father of everything and the very Light of the universe.

After Vesudeva realized that all things originated with this Light; he made it his life's purpose to serve it. It was the Light that called him to the river, to replace the old couple and call his first student, Nestor.

ॐ

Nestor waited on the dock and recalled that night, when he stumbled stoned and wet onto the ferryman's dock; what transpired still filled him with wonder. Although the hour was very late, the ferryman was awake, waiting seated beside a small fire, tending a pot of freshly brewed coffee.

Standing, the ferryman welcomed and offered Nestor a warm blanket. "So you have finally arrived. Sit, have some warm coffee before you become sick. My name is Vesudeva and I have been waiting for you." Sipping coffee, wrapped in the ferryman's woolen blanket, gradually Nestor composed himself. "What? You knew I was coming. How? Did you hear me when I fell into the water trying to climb from the row boat to the dock?"

"Yes. I heard you fall and pull yourself from the water. However, I knew you were coming. Why do you think there was a boat, at this hour by the far side dock? Didn't you consider how the boat happened to be there?"

Mumbling to himself, Nestor replied, "No, I had not thought about how the boat got there or how I would cross the water." It was at this point that Nestor passed out.

so

It was late morning when Nestor awoke. He had a throbbing headache and found himself sleeping in an unfamiliar hut on the dirt floor; wrapped in a woolen blanket and could smell coffee warming on the fire. For a moment Nestor was disoriented, not knowing where he was. Slowly, it all came back to him; the drinking, smoking and bet. Alone, rowing across the river in the middle of the dark night; with only a fire's light on the distant shore to guide him. The fire's light? He had been lucky a strong fire was burning late into the evening. Why did the ferryman tend a fire so late? Usually, by this hour dinner fires were faint embers.

Yet Vesudeva, that was the ferryman's name, said he had been waiting for Nestor. How was that possible? Suddenly, Nestor began to tremble and grow worried. Had he stumbled into the home of a sorcerer? Frightened, Nestor wondered if he would leave this place alive.

Just then Vesudeva entered the hut carrying wild berries and freshly caught river trout. Bending, he spoke, "good, I see you have finally awakened. Have some coffee; while I prepare and cook these fish. Eat some of the berries; it will help your stomach and headache."

9

Sensing reluctance and fear, Vesudeva continued, "don't you think if I intended you harm, I could have pushed you into the river while you slept? Your drunken friends would have thought you drowned in the shifting currents before you could find out anything about the old ferryman."

Suddenly, Nestor became very sober and realized the old man had read his mind. This frightened Nestor even more and he began to wonder how he could get out of the old one's hut before he was harmed?

Smiling Vesudeva offered, "You are free to leave whenever you want."

Then Nestor stood and dashed from the hut: running across the dock; untying the small boat which he used the night before; and rowing toward the far shore as fast as he could.

For months in his head, Nestor heard the old man's laughter. It was a kind, yet gentle, haunting laugh that came from the straw hut as Nestor fled for his life.

∓

Eventually, after much anxiety and jumbled thoughts, Nestor returned frightened to the ferryman's hut. He was convinced that he was going mad and was bewitched. He wanted to beg the old man to lift the spell. Nestor realized something powerful, which he did not fully understand, pulled him to the ferryman.

In the months following his initial nocturnal visit to the ferryman's hut, Nestor's old life changed and gradually fell apart. As he worked in the city, selling carpets from his family store, Nestor was preoccupied and could not get the old man's laughter out of his mind. When Nestor went to the tavern, to drink with his old friends, he could no longer sip the wine or inhale the hashish, without feeling guilty and uncomfortable. Nestor constantly thought about the ferryman and wondered how the old one knew he was coming that night?

When Nestor partially accepted, the ferryman left the boat and kept the fire burning so he would not lose his way or die swimming in the shifting currents, this frightened Nestor even more. Later when Nestor asked the ferryman about all of this, the ferryman laughed a soft reply, "Your heart knows the answer to these questions. Learn to be still and listen. Come, sit beside me by the water and listen to your own inner voice of wisdom."

Then the teacher and student sat on the dock and together began to hear the soft, varied sounds of the river. And as Nestor focused on the music of the river currents, the ferryman softly said, "Go deeper. Imagine yourself as the river that has been traveling through the long, cold night and finally sees the morning sunlight cresting on the horizon. Embrace this Light. Feel its pleasing warmth, bringing life and sunshine to the countryside. You are part of this countryside and find expression drinking in this Light. In turn, give of yourself to the thirsty countryside."

And as Nestor experienced his awakening spiritual Light, in that timeless moment, he began the journey of knowing and learning what he would become and yet always was. He was beside the teacher who reflected Light upon Nestor's inner darkness.

₭   ₭

Each is a confusion of shifting
Thoughts, ideas and desires.
How to make order from these patterns
And understand who you really are?
This is the condition of humanity.

Go deeper. Below the surface water
There is silence and peace.

In these waters, with a little help
You will discover who you really are.

§

The repetitious pattern of daily life
Exists to provide a structure-
To help set the spiritual traveler free.
While the body and every day consciousness is busy
Something finer, more subtle can emerge.

§

— 3 —

Fear as Motivator

Because of our biologic makeup we are fearful. Dangerous things frighten us and we have a strong emotional and physical reaction. This inborn sensitivity has kept the human species alive for millions of years and we are all hardwired to react instantly to perceived danger.

Many human service organizations, governments, and corporations recognize and use the human sensitivity to perceived danger by operating a fear and reward system. This fear and reward methodology, i.e., do as we say and we will reward you or fail to do as we say and we will punish; is very effective in producing predictable outcomes and is efficient in multiple situations. In a sense, institutions within our culture have learned to use our own fear response to motivate and control.

Consider the need for discipline and instant response in a military campaign. Here the fear and reward cycle is easy to view. Follow orders or someone will die. Or in an employment setting, work hard for the corporation, do what management dictates and you will be promoted receiving a higher salary. Conversely, fail to follow orders and you will die or be fired.

More subtle and sometimes not so subtle manipulations of this technique occur throughout our lives in relationships, school and religious training. Basically, do as we like or say and there is a reward. Fail to follow our teaching or wishes- there is a penalty.

When viewing this form of motivation it is helpful to consider the effect. What is the outcome of this manipulation? Many times the individual and the society benefit. Other times, it is the manipulator and the institution who benefit. Within the area of higher studies and religious expression, in order for higher learning to operate there must be no element of fear or compulsion. Fear keeps the higher element from coming forward.

ℤ   ℤ

As the ferryman transported his three passengers across the water, Nestor reminisced and slipped back into that moment of knowing. Through the use of the prayer, Nestor focused inward and returned to that place inside that emanated with the energy of the worlds. This energy was the spark of creation that the ferryman worked with and was the center of Nestor's being. This was the mirror, the ferryman gradually taught Nestor, to wipe clean from the dust of selfish living.

When Nestor was in this place, meditating, united with the Light, he was a beacon unto himself. He was both the question and the answer. Everything stood still. There was no time and space. All that mattered was the Light. This was the life force and the point of all life was to serve harmoniously. This energy was to be used and consulted in daily life. That was the secret and could only be understood and displayed through experience of itself.

In the times that Nestor visited Vesudeva, Nestor realized that much of what he had been taught about life, the world and reality was incomplete. It was a starting place; a foundation upon which to prepare for life in the town where he was born. The fact that this was a beginning, and preparation for something else had never been stated or discussed. Nestor guessed, the reason this instruction was presented in this way was perhaps the instructors were unaware of any other potential.

Learning about daily life was necessary to prepare for the world and learning about higher consciousness was needed to complete the person; fill the inner emptiness and enhance experience about the world. For some, learning about everyday life was enough. For others like Nestor, this preparation left him incomplete and empty. It was this emptiness and unease that Nestor sought to fill nightly with wine and hashish.

As a youngster, the good people of Tajjali had done their very best to fill all the young people's heads, including Nestor, with the things deemed necessary to live. These experiences represented the skills and learning most people thought were necessary to prepare for adult life. Unfortunately, this over emphasis on worldly accomplishment lead to a condition which Vesudeva called, 'world sickness.'

A characteristic of this illness was an unbalanced concern and worry about daily life. There was an ever-present need for comfort and removal of fearful and painful events. When people did not get what they wanted, they did not know how to respond in a healthy manner. People had forgotten that life was more than a physical experience.

Often, learning centered on maxims like these. "Go to school and learn skills necessary to make a living. Enter the army and serve your country. Find a good woman or man and settle down. Raise a family and go to church. Do these things and you will be happy. Fail to follow this path and you will be unhappy."

As he matured into a young man, these were some of the spoken and unspoken rules Nestor struggled with. Very few challenged these maxims and most people went about their lives, unaware of other choices.

With all this well intentioned advice and learning, something still was missing. Growing numbers of young people felt it. They could not explain or define it, but knew that this patterned living left something out. For some, this ideal did not explain the need for excitement or individual expression. Sadly for others, 'this ideal life' could not and did not fill the inner unease and emptiness. So they sought to fill the empty place with alcohol, drugs, and all manner of excitements.

For Nestor it was his inner emptiness that Vesudeva filled with the Light. The Light healed and absorbed the fear instilled by others, and the unease of not knowing how to express oneself amidst the societal choices. The Light helped Nestor to understand that preparation for life was taught by parents, church and schools. How to learn and integrate all of this into a balanced life was learned through higher consciousness, the Light, and inner experience.

ഔ   ഔ

We are born incomplete
So that the Light might fill this emptiness;
And in the process
We might experience who we really are.

ഔ

The hardest battles are not fought in fields,
Or on seas
But within ourselves.
We are the enemy
Who ravages
Every defenseless position.

ഔ

— 4 —

Everything You Need

From a spiritual perspective, each person is born with every-thing they need to make the journey. Each traveler has strengths, abilities, interests and skills that are innate. Overtime, depend-ing upon circumstance and destiny, these skills develop and the course of the life emerges.

The piece that is missing is the intervention of the teacher. In part the teacher exists to show the traveler their own higher, inner capacity and potential. This capacity is displayed through personal spiritual experience.

Through the grace of the Path and teacher's intervention, the dust of 'selfish' living is wiped away and the traveler experiences their own inner potential. It is through this experience that the traveler is shown the goal of their long seeking. The burning is defined and the search has tangible form.

When a soul enters this world it enters with a mission or life plan. As the Source Wills, the soul takes on a physical form so that it might grow, experience, serve, and go and do many things. Yet ultimately, time in this world will have been wasted unless the person grows closer to their higher destiny and the Source.

In all fields of human endeavor, people have different skill sets, aptitudes, strengths and weaknesses. Some people are born to be musicians others are born to parent a large family. While everyone must come to some understanding of their relationship with the Source, people vary in their need to work in this area. Some are content to think about this once per week. Some are content to deny and fight against the world of spirit. Still, others can only accept after they have denied for some time.

In many ways we are like a wild flower. A seed has fallen to the earth and has everything it needs to mature. The seed goes deep into the ground and in the spring reaches up. It is in the sun and rain its destiny will unfold. The flower will help give life to the meadow. Its fragrance will travel on the breeze and bees will drink the nectar; using the nectar to carry out their own individual destiny.

During changing weather patterns, the flower will be tested and its view of the meadow will expand. It has a function and in part- that is the point of the flower's existence.

ຂ   ຂ

During the heat of midday, both Vesudeva and Nestor rested beside the river. They sipped mint tea and ate a meal of berries and vegetable onion stew that Nestor had prepared earlier.

As both men finished eating their lunch, they sat quietly listening to the river. The river's song was the song of life and as you listened to the river, in time you could hear your own song. Once you experienced your own inner song, you could hear the music in all things. Every living thing had its own melody, awareness and energy.

These were some of the mysteries that Vesudeva unlocked for Nestor and as Nestor's inner awareness grew he learned more about self and the world.

In time Vesudeva began to speak. The lesson, what they had been sharing in their moment of silent prayer and attunement, changed to spoken form.

"You see, we all are created like this river for a multitude of purposes. We have a function to serve that is both singular and multilevel. Many people go through their lives and are content with the surface learning. Their world view of the people about them is sufficient. It answers questions and provides a structure in which to express self. Then there are others who for different reasons cannot find expression in this cultural form. They burn for something else. Some of these travelers become our students. Their destiny primarily is a spiritual one."

"One person is not better than another. Each serves a purpose and is part of the Plan. Your responsibility is to uncover who you are and once this has been accomplished help others."

୫

Emil left work early and began walking toward the river. Last night to save time, Emil packed clothing and writing supplies for days of reporting in the country. Later that afternoon, Emil was to meet his old friend Nestor who had arranged the extended interview with Vesudeva. Graciously, Vesudeva had agreed to share some of his teachings with others. The newspaper was running a series of articles on the growing interest in spirituality throughout the river basin.

Emil and Nestor had been mates since they were little ones and Emil was present that night when Nestor left Tajjali Tavern to debunk Vesudeva. After days of waiting, when Nestor finally returned, Emil was one of those who questioned Nestor about his experiences. Today, now four years later, Emil still wondered how the old man hypnotized his friend. Nestor was one of the last people that Emil would have picked to go on a 'God trip.' Nestor was never religious and Emil could not recall a serious conversation other than which girl they wanted between them. To that point, Nestor, like everyone else their age, was focused on the girls, drink and hashish. They all reasoned- at some point

19

they had to find a job, but never really looked past the weekend games.

Emil could not explain Nestor's behavior any other way. When the Senior Newspaper Editor assigned Emil to work with the team on the series about the upsurge in New Age Religions and local holy men and women, Emil saw an opportunity to uncover what really happened to his friend. Emil was prepared to ask Vesudeva directly how he hypnotized and brainwashed his friend.

Realizing there might be some personal danger in this, particularly if the ferryman considered Emil a threat to his control over Nestor, Emil kept his real purpose a secret. On the surface, this encounter was to be a series of questions about the ferryman's teachings. Minimally, Emil wanted to answer the local curiosity about how the ferryman came to work the river and if there was any truth to the rumor of his miraculous healing powers.

ℴ

Emil arrived at the river a few minutes before four o'clock. As he climbed down the river bank, he could see a family of four waiting beside the dock. They were carrying gifts and provisions. Emil guessed they were visiting family or friends on the far side of the river. As the ferryman and the raft drew past mid-river and closer to the dock, Emil got in line with the others. Not knowing how many travelers were carried on each trip, he did not want to miss his turn.

As the ferryman drew closer, Emil recognized his old friend steering the raft toward the dock. It was not Vesudeva. Their meeting would have to wait. Happy to be met by his old friend, excitedly Emil began to shout and wave and after a few moments, Nestor looked up from the water to judge his distance from the dock and saw his friend. Nestor quickly waved back, then refocused attention on guiding the raft. He steered upriver and using the flow, he angled into the dock.

As Emil watched Nestor skillfully handle the raft, he wondered, so the old one has his student working for him? Does Nestor get paid? Probably not. A learning exercise of some sort. Yes, there had been many changes since Nestor began visiting the ferryman. Many of which, like this one troubled Emil. Emil feared Nestor was being taken advantage of. Emil wondered just how far Nestor would go under the ferryman's direction. At first, when Nestor refused to visit the tavern this troubled Emil. He missed his old friend and the fun nights they had together. What bothered him even more than not being with his friend was the explanation Nestor offered. He claimed to have found something more important. The tavern now made him sad and he had learned to hear his own inner song which this activity drowned out. Emil could not understand what Nestor was talking about. Together they sang many drinking songs and there was nothing finer than having a young lady ready for your bed.

Also since meeting the ferryman, Nestor had not missed a day of work at the carpet stall and claimed to enjoy getting up daily and entering in the commerce of the world. Nestor stated, each had to contribute to the good of all.

From the dock watching Nestor smile, as he guided the raft closer, Emil thought, "Sadly, our poor boy has been brainwashed and is reciting ideas that are not even his own."

℘　　℘

That which you have been Given
Is enough for the Journey.

℘

Remember, you have within
a magic wand. Pick it up!
Learn how to use it.

— 5 —
An Original Life

Each life is a dichotomy: both unique and the same. Additionally, each life is an original expression of the creative potential of the universe. During the course of life, each traveler has to create a balance between those parts that are universal and those that are deeply personal.

Within the parameters of free will choice travelers are to create their own destiny. The answer to the question, "What is the purpose of life," is an answer that the traveler works out and creates themselves. On one level, the point of the journey is for the traveler to experience different things, learn and more fully understand their individual role in the universe. To this end, each traveler grows in understanding of the Source and is a creator within specific areas of their life.

The great philosophies, religions and teachers exist to help the traveler make decisions that have a personal impact. Each has a set of potential learning experiences and talents, which are to be made manifest in the world. Then we react on a day to day basis and these reactions help create our own unique journey.

Each person comes into this world with specific talents and a life plan which they help to create. During the course of their life, events occur that are beyond one's control and others that we help create; in both sets of circumstances, the individual has the opportunity to react, grow and learn. This learning and movement is in relation to that which they wish to become. Each makes choices and creates daily. Other times, events occur and we react to them; learning and building from each experience.

This world is a giant bazaar and there are vendors with all kinds of experiences, goods and deceptions. Within certain limits, you can pick and choose and spend your time as you like. This experience of exploration, pleasure and learning is for the most part up to you. In the main, depending upon inclination and ability, you can do as you like.

There has never been and there will never be someone exactly like you. You are an original expression of the Source and with each movement and experience grow closer to your ultimate destiny. Each is destined to be a governor of a vast spiritual kingdom and share in Kingship with the Source.

The person who has completed the journey while in this body, has learned to unlock their latent spiritual potential. This hidden capacity is a byproduct of a higher state of consciousness. The level and variation of spiritual talent is individual and dependent upon their specific life journey and how they are to influence and help others.

                                                        ₨   ₨

Vesudeva prepared bedding for their visitor. He carried meadow grass that had been drying in the sun and arranged it below the window on the far side of the hut. Here the evening breeze was coolest and their visitor could fall asleep to the serenade of the river as it made its way through the night.

Vesudeva agreed to the interview, intuitively understanding Nestor's unspoken desire to help his friend. Nestor was overjoyed with Vesudeva's response and hoped this interchange would do more than help Emil's newspaper career. Secretly, Nestor hoped this opportunity to learn about the Teaching would in time lead Emil to the Light.

Vesudeva understood all this but also knew that each traveler had their own time and it was only grace that allowed a traveler to accept the Light. The inner burning could only be stilled at the right time, in the right place and with the right people. Vesudeva was a servant of this Light and offered teaching as he was directed.

Stopping his work, Vesudeva paused and looked out the window and as he focused upon the river, he felt that other part of himself coming awake. Slowly, he could feel the energy emanating from within. This was the energy of creation, of which at his center this was a small spark, and as this spark activated it expanded and joined with the energy all about him. Now Vesudeva was fully conscious and connected to all living things. And as Vesudeva watched the water, as it flowed, his soul drank of the Infinite. In that moment, Vesudeva had become a drop in the river, flowing home.

ɛɔ

Nestor and Emil spoke as Nestor guided the ferry toward the far shore. "I'm so happy that you could spend some time with us. Perhaps, as you write your article, you will benefit personally from this experience."

Emil replied, "Yes, circumstances certainly seem to have worked out. I'm looking forward to spending this time with you as well as learning more about Vesudeva's Teaching. Hopefully this piece will help spread his work."

Nestor probed for a more personal response. "Aren't you the least bit curious about what you might learn?"

"What do you mean learn? Sure, I'm curious and I come into this story with an open mind, like any good reporter. But learn, I don't know what you mean?"

"Perhaps, what you learn will challenge your own view of life and the way you look at the world? Vesudeva's teachings have a way of doing that, you know."

"Well, we will see. I just don't want to get ahead of myself."

❧

Vesudeva brewed fresh mint leaves for tea which he had just picked from the garden. Over the years, Vesudeva learned to keep an outdoor fire going throughout the day and evening. Many times, travelers needed to warm themselves beside a cozy fire before continuing their journey. Also, the conversation around a fire helped Vesudeva learn about the outside world and, as circumstances dictated, offer a kind word for the weary traveler.

Their table was nestled beneath the shade of one of the large willows that lined the river. Their meal was to consist of honey with their tea, fresh raspberries and a loaf of wheat bread baked by one of the ferry travelers. Often Vesudeva accepted useful items and food as payment for ferrying travelers across the water.

Earlier from his quiet contemplation and reflecting the Light, Vesudeva realized that these next few days were part of a dance that was being orchestrated from another level. The upcoming exchange would hold importance for many and this was only part of the message he had received.

❧

As Nestor guided the raft into the dock, Vesudeva was standing there to greet the passengers. After helping the family of four safely step from the raft to dry land, Vesudeva called to his guest.

"Emil, I am so pleased that you have come for a visit. Nestor has told me much about you and I am happy to share what we speak about. Come inside. Put your belongings away. Then we will have lunch."

And as the raft rested alongside the dock, Nestor secured a rope around the pylon. Then Vesudeva stepped onto the raft and continued speaking. "Come Emil. Let me help you with your belongings." Before Emil could reply, Vesudeva reached down and lifted up Emil's luggage.

Then all three began walking toward the hut. The fact that Vesudeva greeted them on the dock and carried luggage surprised Emil. As they walked, Emil thought, "A holy man who carries other people's luggage. Vesudeva is either very clever or just being gracious. Either way, I must be on my guard."

૭૦   ૭૦

Like a captive bird
The soul sings,
Remembering its home.

It is precisely for this song,
The bird is caged.

૭૦

He is master
Who reigns supreme
In their own kingdom.

૭૦

— 6 —

Spiritual Energy

Within the universe, there is a life giving and creative energy. This supra-energy permeates all of the many worlds, universes and dimensions. It can be called the Light, the life force, the Logos, the Holy Spirit, God or the Source.

Deity extends a part of itself into this world of forms. Deity simply is and has created the universe, in part to express itself and share in the experience of creation. Each of us has a small piece, or spark of this wondrous element within. This is the center of our soul and has its own creative potential. This potential is used daily, in part to help create our physical body, our conscious awareness and the world we live in.

For some time, our scientists have suspected this force or universal energy existed. From their perspective it is a logical assumption and many have begun to explore the nature of this energy, its characteristics and potential. In our time, one might say, science has identified a 'God.' From their perspective it just makes logical sense.

According to Sufi tradition, since the very beginning, individuals have been given the responsibility of guarding and directing this multi-level energy. Daily it is projected into this realm, yiedling ideas and influences. In part, this Force is a nutrient; it enables and without it our world would cease to exist.

This Force and the Teaching are the same. The Teaching is an aspect of this wonderful life giving and loving energy. During the course of study, the spiritual traveler learns to become one with this energy and life force.

The guardians and servants of this energy and Path are the living teachers. They exist in all traditions and walks of life. In our time, we are experiencing a more public exploration and general inquiry into the meaning of spiritual science.

You have a piece or aspect of this wondrous treasure within. Your job is to uncover this spiritual center beneath your many layers of consciousness; refine and use it in your daily life.

ɛɔ   ɛɔ

Emil waited for the mint tea to cool, nibbling on a fresh picked wild raspberry. Gazing about, he thought to himself, the berry's sweetness fits the beauty and tranquility of this spot. The original ferryman was wise to settle here. Here the water was calm, and with a sturdy bamboo raft the distance between shores was manageable. As the sunlight filtered through the shade trees, there was enough light for the day's activity. At night, Emil judged, the river breeze brought refreshing coolness.

For the ferryman, who was welcoming his guest and seated directly across the table from Emil, this moment was an interlude, a time to rest between the last two trips of the day.

Emil took a sip of tea and then breathed deeply. He was getting nervous sitting here with the ferryman. Slow breathing helped Emil manage his anxiety and control his heartbeat. Again, Emil took another long slow breath and inhaled the river's sweet fragrant mixture of plant, fish and animal life. This further relaxed him. As Emil listened to the sound of the river and its sweet lullaby over the countryside, he found his eyes beginning to close. In that moment, Emil almost fell asleep but caught himself. Fearfully, he inwardly cautioned, "Be vigilant. While you are dosing, the ferryman might take this opportunity to extend control into your mind."

Smiling, the ferryman looked directly at Emil and softly spoke. "I hope you take this opportunity with us to rest and further explore your own inner awareness. Here in this quiet spot we are fortunate. Natural surroundings provide us with an opportunity to explore the inner journey. Here there is great natural peace and contrasting activity. In the life of the river, with its dichotomy of peace and activity through the country-side, many travelers have found other aspects of themselves. Observing of what is taking place around self can serve as a mirror or way to journey inward into one's own soul."

"Please finish eating. I need to check the raft for the next 2 runs. My absence will give you both time to catch up, rest and get settled. Perhaps, later tonight around the fire we can talk about the inner journey."

"Nestor, help make Emil comfortable. See if there is any-thing else he would like to eat. Show him where he will sleep. Perhaps you might fish for a late night snack?"

Then the ferryman stood and made his way toward the dock, leaving the two friends to chat with each other.

ɛ꙰

When the ferryman was out of hearing range, Nestor ques-tioned, "What do you think of him? Is he what you expected?"

Emil paused for a moment to gather his thoughts, then replied, "I must confess, no, he is not. I'm not really sure what I expected a holy man to look like. Perhaps, wearing a long beard and flowing robes? He reminds me of a kindly old man. Like some one's grandfather. Yet there is something else. It's difficult to explain. Almost like an air of peace about him. Yes. That's more like it. A peaceful, loving energy coming from him."

Nestor paused for a moment before replying, wondering if he should hold back and decided, in part he would. "Yes. There is something different about Vesudeva and you have perceived it."

"What do you mean perceived it?"

"Perceiving is different than feeling. It is deeper. In time you may further understand this. For now I am happy you are here. Come let me show you where you will sleep. Take the time to refresh yourself. Go to the river for a swim, while I will try to catch us a late night snack."

∞

As Emil laid out his sleeping bag, through the hut's window, he watched Nestor casting a fishing line. Certainly Nestor looked happy and full of energy. In some ways this was a different person than he had known. For sure, Nestor's anxiousness and intensity, which came across as seriousness seemed to be replaced with joy. Fishing for his own food, Nestor was full of energy and seemed to enjoy working the river raft.

Somehow, Emil would never have imagined that his boyhood friend would find peace or contentment in these activities. Certainly not the Nestor of the drinking and party games. Was this a hidden aspect of his friend's personality or was this behavior engineered by a sinister force? Had Vesudeva hypnotized and brainwashed Nestor into accepting these duties as a learning exercise of sorts? Emil had to wonder.

∞

Each time Vesudeva pulled the bamboo oar through the water he was repeating the Holy Name. The Name had become his friend; and just as he took in a deep breath- he spoke the first part of the Name. While exhaling, slowly, he spoke the second part of the Name and with a soft voice caressed each letter. In this way, both his body and spirit were one; steering the raft across the river for the last pick-up.

30

His physical motion and mental activity, by repeating the Name, became a prayer that united the physical, mental and spiritual. In motion with the river, Vesudeva and the raft moved effortlessly.

         ဆ   ဆ

We are travelers through the many worlds.
Our stay in this one
Is like an afternoon by the ocean
With family and friends.
Let us embrace and enjoy this hour.
For when the sun sets
We must continue onward;
Traveling- making our way to the next place.

ဆ

While in this world
The soul is bound
By the chains of daily life.
One day the soul shall soar free.
Until then-
Enjoy the momentary flight.

ဆ

On summer nights I hear a whisper to walk outside.
In time, I stop to feel the cool breeze caress my face.
Slowly, I dissolve into the infinity about me-
And become a particle on the wind.
A warm glow guides me
And I am again
One with the Cosmos.

ဆ

— 7 —

The Plan

One traveler at a time, humanity is evolving to a higher state of consciousness. This evolution is both individual and collective. As a race of people we are all reaching Higher. This evolution is purposeful and directed so that it may be attained.

To help safeguard this Plan there is a hierarchy of servants who work on many levels. Collectively humanity has a potential and destiny. Many of the holy books speak about this potential. These references are part allegorical and part literal.

In the Plan, each traveler or soul has a distinct role. In part, that is what this life is about. To discover how you fit into the world, using your physical, mental and spiritual skills. The world needs travelers who are doing what they can to make things better for them selves and others.

In each day, there are many opportunities to reach higher and fulfill your individual destiny or Plan. Simply ask yourself before doing something that you are uncertain about; if this action will bring you closer or further distance you from your higher destiny and the Source. Learn to wait for an answer. You can do this. Slowly you will begin to awaken and hear your own inner capacity. Follow this voice. This inner voice and its wisdom are aligned with the higher destiny of the universe.

When you leave this world and continue on, in some respects

the next phase is similar to this one. In each place, you express who you are in relation to the universe and what you wish to accomplish. Each is a ray of Light that has come from a vast and glorious Sun. It has been sent out into the universe to experience itself in many forms and dimensions. Growing stronger in wisdom and service to the glorious Sun- of which it is an expression. One day it finds itself going home to shine, along with the other suns, upon the universe.

And because this journey is of spirit, there is no real time or space in relation to the Divine. As the Source Wills, this journey may be accomplished in an instant or in a thousand lifetimes. It may be accomplished once or over and over again. It is all up to you.

Each day when we close our eyes and align ourselves with the Source; through the Light we are illuminating the darkness within, and become a sun shining the Light unto ourselves and others.

In this we serve, individually and collectively: helping complete the Plan for humanity.

ಸಾ   ಸಾ

It was early evening. Vesudeva had completed the final run of the day, and as the sun set in the western sky, the river valley was aglow with a brilliant display of colors, dancing across the sky. There were different shades of orange, yellow, red and blue combining, creating a patchwork of colors.

And as the evening arrived, a cool breeze flew across the water and Vesudeva, Nestor and Emil warmed themselves by the outdoor fire. Across the flames, each was holding a branch that was skewered through a freshly caught and cleaned river trout.

Having been accustomed to others cooking; Emil felt awkward in this task, and Vesudeva showed Emil how to hold the trout over a part of the fire that burned evenly, with low, strong flames. When it was time to turn the trout, Vesudeva nodded to Emil. Happily Vesudeva chatted about the passengers he met earlier in the day and on the final run. Keeping a careful eye on both his and Emil's fish turning, indicating as required.

When the cooking was done, all were seated at the table waiting for the trout to cool; and Vesudeva questioned Emil, "So you have come to learn about our teaching and to share it in the newspaper?"

Emil replied, "Yes. I hope that by spending time with you and Nestor, I might learn what he finds so useful in what you talk about. Coincidently, our newspaper is doing a series on New Age Teachers and I thought, with your permission, I would write an article to share with others. What do you say to that?"

Vesudeva smiled and indicated, "You are here, are you not? That is my answer." For an instant, this reply stopped Emil. Not fully understanding: if this was a yes or a no. Cautiously Emil continued, "Since you have agreed, when will lessons begin?"

Vesudeva replied, "The lessons began the moment you decided to join us and learn. From that moment, you have been thinking, wondering what kind of teaching would appeal to your old friend enough to take him away from the tavern life. Similarly from the moment you arrived, you have been observing, considering and evaluating. Is this not learning?"

Somewhat confused, Emil offered, "But this is not learning as I know it. This is not what I anticipated. Where is the classroom or direct instruction?"

Vesudeva answered, "Travelers expect to learn only in a formal, classroom situation. Yet the Teaching rarely presents itself within this form. It is more organic. Life is the great classroom. Everything around us interacts with us and teaches on many levels. Travelers forget this and expect learning to occur in a form that is familiar. A classroom, with a fixed period and a teacher who is the source of knowledge. Or a church, synagogue, or mosque with a designated leader. Most students are used to waiting for something important to happen or be said."

"Yet in our way of thinking and learning, something important is always happening. However, to understand and comprehend, the student must change the way they look at things. To view reality in this manner, often, it is not a matter of adding but removing something. Preconceived ideas and attitudes about learning must be removed, so something else might come forward -higher consciousness."

Seeing the confusion in Emil's face, Vesudeva paused for a moment. Inwardly, Vesudeva smiled to himself and continued, "Since you are our guest, it is unfair to make you feel uncomfortable your first night with us. Yet this unease is a good sign. It shows you are listening, thinking and trying to learn."

"Tonight I will offer a lesson in a more standard fashion. Consider this trout that is cooling on your plate. Who created this fish and for what purpose? Had the fish ever considered that one day it would become an evening meal? Or while spawning, did this trout consider that it might give birth to hundreds of others? Does this fish have consciousness or awareness of its life purpose? If so, where will this conscious awareness go after the trout's flesh fills your stomach? Where did Nestor learn to fish? How did his ancestors learn this skill? Where did all this trout knowledge come from? Also, how did travelers acquire tools necessary to cook and clean this creature?"

"Just as there was a plan to bring this fish to our dinner plate that involved the interplay of many across thousands of years, what of the other thousands of trout that do not make it to this table? What part do they play in the continued life of the river valley? Different philosophies and world views explain this phenomenon. Science indicates these fish are part of a larger eco-system. More are born each year than are required to help the species survive. When they are minnows, some will be eaten by larger fish. Others will mature to have young of their own, and countless others will pass on due to disease and the fisherman's hook."

"Some people see in this multi-level activity of the trout: confusion, happenstance, or survival of the fittest. Depending upon individual preference: it is either a scientific, religious or philosophical view. Yet no matter the individual view of the onlooker a fish reality exists. For surely, this trout lived, swam in the river and its passing will provide sustenance for us tonight."

"In all this activity, is there not a plan of sorts? Consider who or what created the river valley, this fire, the learned capacity to catch dinner, so you might live another day to consider this question or dismiss it as unimportant. Yet, whatever you do with this opportunity to learn, is this learning impacted by either Nestor's view or my own? And does it really matter what we think, believe or experience in relation to this? Is different energy engendered when many people believe the same thing?"

Vesudeva paused, looked directly at Emil and offered, "And if it doesn't really matter, these questions, would you be here to learn something about all of this? One last thought before you bite into that fine trout which Nestor skillfully caught and cleaned. It has almost completely cooled down from the fire, ready for eating. Consider this, if there is a plan of sorts for this fish, would there not be a plan for higher life forms like you and I? If so, what would that plan be? Also, in relation to this plan, what might be your individual responsibility?"

৪৩

As Emil slowly separated the trout meat from the numerous small bones and took a bite of the sweet flesh, his head was spinning. Gazing into the firelight which illuminated Vesudeva's smiling face, Emil wondered, "Has Vesudeva just scolded me in some way?"

Slowly, his head stopped spinning and Emil considered, the lesson about a fish's life. Seemingly there was much to consider. Yet who even thinks about these things? In this lesson where was the practicality? Also, something else seemed to be going on around the fire. It was difficult to fully comprehend, but there seemed to be an energy emanating from Vesudeva that filled the open space around the camp fire with a soft, golden glow. Gradually, this light reached out and embraced all who were present, with a peaceful loving, caress.

Then, Emil's head began to spin again, and he wondered what this energy was all about?

ꙮ   ꙮ

What acorn needs to question
The reason for its existence?
O man, why can't you understand
The mysteries of life and death?

Are you no better, than this little seed?

ꙮ

When faced with the sunset
It is easy to forget the morning.
Yet, both exist
And follow one another.

ꙮ

Just as water must undergo change to become snow,
So, we must undergo a process of alteration.

Slowly, the world of the senses
Must be taught to give-way

To the world of the soul,
Then, the change is complete.

ಐ

— 8 —
Finding a Path

Each person's journey is individual and, at the same time, on an inner level, collective. Meaning that the sequence of learning experience varies according to the person, the time and their higher not emotional needs. This sequence is established by the Teaching, the teacher, and the path. It is a sequence that originates from another dimension; has Baraka or grace attached to it and operates within its own rules.

In our time many are searching for a path that will bring them fulfillment. In this respect the search is similar to other cultures and times. However because of the present societal emphasis upon the role of the individual and the importance of individual assertion; many believe they can pick and choose a path like they are shopping for a new car: they have a list of specific requirements and are looking for the right deal or fit.

Many seek a path that will be fulfilling in a manner as defined by them. They want learning experiences to "make them whole, peaceful, happy and connected to the larger universe." People are free to want these things and establish their own learning criteria. However, authentic paths do not necessarily adhere to this structure. The path has its own criteria that the student must meet. The path exists to fulfill a spiritual function and is secondarily concerned about the student's emotional fulfillment.

In this understanding the traveler is usually lacking, often insisting upon emotional stimuli that a true path cannot meet and unaware there may be other criteria necessary for learning. For example, the path exists to teach the student how to quiet emotional stimuli and bring forward inner latent capacity. This capacity will not operate under conditions where the student is overly concerned about feeling happy or peaceful. For a time, the student must be able to push aside this need for specific stimuli. Usually, beginning students do not realize they have defined their search mostly in emotional terms.

Because this need may not be conscious or the student may be unable to minimize their need for emotional excitement without further work; what is generally provided by authentic paths is education about the matter. For some beginners, there have been instances where this criterion was not used, however, statements like this may be offered instead of instruction. "You are not ready for what we have to offer. You cannot control your need for emotional fulfillment and must learn to minimize this need before we can work with you."

Instead of fully examining this diagnosis, what happens is an emotional response of being 'rejected.' Yet this simply points out a requirement necessary for entrance into study.

In all complex learning systems, the entrance criteria are subtle and refined; ultimately set by the Teacher and dependent upon what is being taught. Consider the skills necessary for the surgeon before he can do 'brain surgery,' and what educational preparation is required before working on a human brain. Here the requirements are just as complex.

When the student is ready, the teacher will call to the student. At this point, the student will feel a need to present himself for admittance. All prospective students are observed for the necessary qualities. This evaluation is ongoing and occurs on many levels. Usually the prospective student is unaware it is occurring.

Because we are dealing with the 'original classroom without walls,' students can be observed and evaluated at a great distance. Most often, it is not as mysterious as this and the evaluation occurs while the prospective student is in close proximity. Prospective students question what they can do or how they should occupy themselves while waiting to begin formal study:

- Examine assumptions about readiness for this type of learning.

- Develop sincerity concerning motives and why one is interested in higher consciousness.

- Lead a balanced life, fulfilling the minimum requirements necessary for the social structure in which you live.

- Consider that much of your responses to this endeavor are emotion/excitement laden and may be the door that is in your own way.

- Familiarize yourself with the body of work by Idries Shah or any other teacher who appeals to you. In this age of communication, all teachers have created preparatory materials for prospective students.

- Associate with people who have something to offer about the inner journey. These people will present themselves as ordinary and easily fit into the present social structure. The type of person you can bring home for dinner without concern- they are not 'strange.'

- Pray morning and evening to fulfill your higher destiny and the higher destiny of the universe. Talk to your Higher self and talk to God about your life and journey.

41

- Remember in this matter it is a question of love. The lovers who wish to serve are accepted. Love is never an easy path.

After reviewing this list of requirements, the traveler may become discouraged and wonder, "Is it worth all this trouble? Surely there must be an easier way." But these guidelines are just to get things started! Be aware that this endeavor requires total commitment.

In this journey, it is a matter of burning love. Those who reach journey's end are those who have to travel. For them there is no other choice. They must reach the object of their love or perish.

୨୦   ୨୦

Vesudeva was working outside. Preparing the fire to burn throughout the night, he stoked the embers and rebuilt the outer fire wall. Next he checked the bamboo raft to make sure it was secured to the dock that rested alongside their straw hut. Finally, Vesudeva sat down on the dock, closed his eyes and began his evening meditation. Turning inward, he slowly repeated the prayer of submission, "O Lord, I surrender myself to You." Then he caught and embraced the Light as it came from the Pole and in turn projected the Light across the land to his students, friends and many travelers through the darkness. This was the Light of the universe and magically watered all the flowers in his garden and helped bring forth life for another day.

୨୦

Inside the ferryman's hut, resting, Emil and Nestor were preparing to sleep. The two friends needed to share more of their feelings and expectations.

Nestor spoke first. "I am so happy to have you here. Finally meeting my teacher. What do you think of him? Have you formed any further impressions?"

42

Emil could see that Nestor was truly happy to have him visit and at that moment felt the deep joy of their friendship. Softly Emil answered, "Like a good reporter, I have been keeping notes in my workbook from which to write an article. But to answer your question, no, Vesudeva is not what I expected. He is kind, gentle and seems to be truly friendly."

"At this point, I must play the role of skeptical reporter and I am not fully prepared to either accept or reject. However, I'm not sure how to say this, but again there seems to be an aura of peaceful energy about him. I cannot fully put this in words and it is the second time today I have felt this; when he was speaking by the fire, for a moment I thought I felt a loving energy reach out toward me. I do not know how else to describe it and when I looked at Vesudeva, he was smiling as if to say, "Now. Put that into your article.""

Pausing before speaking, Nestor replied, "So again, you felt it? I must say, I am a bit surprised."

"What do you mean 'felt' it? Also, why would you be surprised?"

"Frankly, although I am pleased you have come to learn about Vesudeva, in my heart, I wondered if you would give this opportunity a fair chance and if you were suited for this learning. I prayed you were but inwardly wondered. Being able to perceive the baraka is a very good sign."

"Now, I don't know if I should be offended? The heathen who is incapable of learning, is that what you really thought?"

"I did not mean to offend. What is important is that you are here, trying to learn and are able to perceive the teaching."

Emil's feelings were still hurt by Nestor's statement, so Emil pressed harder. "Why did you think I could not learn from Vesudeva? You know this hurts a little. Aren't I good enough?"

"Please, I did not mean to offend. It was my fear that this would not work. I wanted this opportunity to work for you and prayed that it would. Nothing would please me more than to have my old friend join in the journey. Frankly, this teaching is not for everyone. Most people cannot feel the energy and inner caress of the Light. It is too subtle. Do you understand?"

"No. I don't know what you mean."

"You said it yourself. You felt that while being with Vesudeva, a loving, kind energy was reaching out toward you. This was not imagination. This is the inner teaching. When this aspect of consciousness is awakened the real learning begins. Now, do you follow?"

"Nestor, I think I will need more time with all of this. Thank you again for arranging this for me. Now, I am tired and must get some sleep."

"Emil, I am truly happy that you have come. I too must sleep, but before sleeping, must pray and meditate. Goodnight old friend." Then Nestor sat up, closed his eyes and focused inward.

Automatically, Emil replied, "Good night," but remained awake wondering what Nestor was praying and meditating about. Also, Emil was still a little hurt by the 'holier than thou' attitude that seemed to be flying about, but tried not to over react.

∽

After a time, finally, Emil fell asleep. Outside their hut, the peaceful river water sang a lullaby to the countryside, and through sleep, Emil's excitement, hurt, and anger faded. Meanwhile, Vesudeva continued reflecting the Light across the land and watering the souls of near and distant travelers.

While sleeping Emil entered a dream phase.

Emil found himself seated atop a high mountain peak. He was robed in a white, shimmering cloth, seated with legs crossed, eyes closed, in a classic meditative posture. It was late evening and the dark sky was aglow with countless stars. Each star sparkled in the dark blue night and emitted rays of light that pulsed with a loving, peaceful energy.

As Emil meditated he could feel energy within himself grow stronger and purposeful. Slowly this energy began to expand and reach out and absorb the part that was Emil. Emil was still there, a part of his consciousness remained, but another part had taken over and was continuing to expand, reaching further outward.

And as Emil pulsed with this energy, which was the same energy that emanated from all the evening stars, he felt himself rise upward and take his place amongst them. In a twinkling of an eye, Emil had become a star to light and brighten the evening sky.

Then as Emil looked back toward the mountain peak, he saw himself still meditating and was one both with that aspect which was earth bound and that aspect that was the Light of Creation.

Both aspects were the same and Emil stayed in this place. The meditating Emil was joined by two other white robed figures. Then these three figures joined their Lights and stayed in this place of union, joy, wonderment and service.

₱

All the time that Emil slept, enjoying this vision, Vesudeva continued to reflect the Light across the land and to his students

₱   ₱

In some respect, part of our lives is spent waiting like passengers in a train station. Some pass the time by studying the people around them. Others engage in conversation, working on their computers, speaking on cell phones, reading or sleeping. Some busy themselves with their work schedule, while others consider the mechanics of engine and cars.

Rare is the individual who can grasp the workings of an entire transportation system and how it was created by the collective energy of thousands of people over hundreds of years. Rare is the individual who can describe how the system serves as a source of social, political and economic activity for a region or nation.

Rarer still is the individual who can foresee a disaster and intervene by altering factors and harmonizing their effect. This view of the function of things and the capacity to modify factors is called by some the higher consciousness. It is the birthright of humanity and is available if you search and are taught to use it.

∾

Over the years, many realize school and learning is not the same thing. While some grow to love learning, often school is dull and repetitious.

School is a preparation for life: while learning is what life is about.

∾

No one believes unless they have proof.
This proof must be in the form of personal experience.

May your seeking be rewarded
With the caress of Higher Knowledge.

∾

— 9 —

What You Learn

While on the path, what exactly is it you learn? How is this different than other forms of learning?

From the very beginning, the traveler is taught that there is an underlying reality in all events, and through proper training at certain times it may be perceived. This perception is then used to fulfill the higher potential or destiny of any given situation.

The physical world or world of forms is supported by the world of spirit. The physical is an extension of this unseen world and exists so humanity can fulfill their higher destiny. Each traveler enters the world of forms for many reasons. Yet each reason is connected to a higher reality and the traveler 'fumbles around in the dark' unless he or she learns to connect with it. The ladder which allows the traveler to connect is religion and spiritual learning. The path and teaching is the core of this reality.

According to the mystic view, humanity suffers from 'world sickness,' and the teaching provides the cure to help the traveler see reality. Most people live their entire lives attached to ideas, possessions and other people. These things to the exclusion of others fill their consciousness. While it is good to be concerned about the things of the world and involved in making things betters for others, there is a point at which this orientation leads you away from the higher, lasting reality. A balance must be maintained between the physical and spiritual.

In this endeavor, it is a matter of degree and attitude. With the proper guidance the traveler learns to participate in the world and inwardly withdraw attachment from the world. While the traveler may go to work everyday, work hard and try to help others, a part of him remains 'sacred' and attached to the Light.

It is the function of the Teacher to help the traveler develop this internal aspect that is always connected to the Light.

For most people, their world view is composed of precon- ceived ideas, beliefs and emotional reactions to situations. Part of the purpose of any culture or society is to formulate a set of guiding principles, which are spread to others who then form an affinity with these beliefs, guiding their daily life to some de- gree. Over time, if the culture or society is to thrive, these beliefs and principles grow stronger and become operating principles. Rarely are these operating principles challenged by the people who follow them. They are accepted as "just the way things are." Yet these beliefs are subject to deterioration and 'hardening;' fail- ing to be updated as necessary. As the members of a society grow old and younger people of the new generation take their place in it, often this is a driving force behind any challenges to existing beliefs or mores. Some of these beliefs may have been instituted as a way to control others or limit the potential of spe- cific groups and eventually this is questioned as well.

Now this grouping of ideas, beliefs and emotional reactions come together to form our world view or the way we face the world. In spiritual terminology, it is called the commanding self: the way we operate daily. In this state, we reluctantly ac- cept criticism or views different than our own. Psychology has termed part of the commanding self 'intellect,' which tries to rea- son things out based upon facts that have been taught, observed and accepted based upon collective societal experience.

From the mystical perspective, it is precisely this consciousness which needs to be pushed aside or suspended momentarily to let other ideas in. Most often it is the intellect that is the door and stands in the way of seeing what is actually in front of you, and blocks the spiritual, higher impulse from operating.

Consider a culture that is based upon commerce and amassing as much personal material wealth as possible. Decisions in this culture will be based upon guiding principles that increase individual and collective wealth. Ideas that target different areas of society, like social services, will be looked upon as less important, and not part of this original, guiding principle. In our society of commercial wealth, what individuals think about and how they examine possibilities will be influenced by this commercial ideal. When individuals do not use this principle to examine events or potentials they may feel 'guilty' or become confused. They almost certainly will be viewed as different or 'strange' by the majority of people.

Gradually the traveler learns to examine assumptions, in order to see exactly what is present, not what is believed to be present. By temporarily suspending the commanding self, the traveler learns to see the reality of the situation and what is beyond the situation, or the 'big picture.'

In order to do this, one has to understand when ideas and beliefs have been engineered (indoctrinated) or when they are inherent to people's needs. Keep in mind, there is nothing wrong with having a commercial view and looking at events in this way. This view becomes a hindrance only when it prevents other things from operating, or you find it does not adequately explain how you look at the world and feel about it. Inwardly, you know there must be something more. So, it is possible to pursue the commercial view, and still allow this "something more" to guide you in connecting with the spiritual.

Within the framework of religions, we find many systems

that state we are the only true path. Yet other paths exist. In this situation, is it a matter of indoctrination or belief; as opposed to the reality of not seeing the true potential of the situation?

ॐ   ॐ

Vesudeva was ferrying the early morning travelers across the river. He enjoyed the day's first run the most; as the sun crests through the trees and greets the new day. Over the last few years, this river and surrounding valley had become his home. Travelers had different names for this strong, vibrant body of water. Vesudeva's favorite was "Lady Velo." After the passing of his wife, this river was now a partner. Sometimes the river sang just like a lover. Other times it roared like a hurt and angry wife.

This morning the bamboo raft was full. The raft at 6 × 18 feet was just the right size to withstand the strong current and maneuver easily. At this hour, a group of four farmers carried fresh produce to the 'Grand Open Market.' The raft was sitting low in the water, with the farmers and their load of vegetables packed in hand made reed baskets. Vesudeva pulled hard, turning on the outboard engines, to propel on a steady course.

Later after the return trip, Nestor agreed to do both midday runs so that Emil and Vesudeva could sit uninterrupted and talk. It was time for Emil to formally begin the interview and gather information for the newspaper article. Turning the paddle to steer, Vesudeva smiled to himself, as he pondered all the things the young reporter still had to consider to make his "newspaper article" complete.

ॐ

When Emil awoke the sun had been up for nearly two hours. He felt refreshed and filled with energy. Earlier, Nestor awoke with Vesudeva and helped plan the day's activity. Both discussed how the day would proceed. Who would make the runs and prepare the meals. Emil was a guest and this status dictated no work assignment. If Emil volunteered to help that would be permitted, however, rules of hospitality dictated no direct involvement.

Hearing Emil stir, Nestor inquired, "How did you sleep? When you are ready come outside by the fire. There is coffee and biscuits."

Emil called back, "First let me go down to the river and wash and refresh myself. Then I will join you. It certainly is a beautiful day."

When Emil returned from the river he inquired, "Where is Vesudeva? I see the raft is already gone. Is he out on the river?"

"Yes. Vesudeva took the early runs and will be back by noon. At that point if you are ready Vesudeva expects you both can begin the interview." Emil replied, "You know I don't remember the last time I slept so well. I am refreshed, happy and full of energy. I guess river life appeals to me? This day promises to be extraordinary."

Nestor smiled and offered Emil coffee and a biscuit. Which Emil took energetically and sat down. Then Nestor filled Emil in on the day's plan.

⁊ᴏ

It was midday. Nestor replaced Vesudeva and was out on the river ferrying passengers. By this time, their fares usually consisted of travelers visiting or returning from a family visit. In this grouping there was an elderly man and a married couple with a young toddler. In contrast, later in the day the runs typically filled with merchants and farmers.

Vesudeva was finishing a bowl of onion and trout stew Nestor prepared earlier. While Vesudeva digested lunch, Emil reviewed his notes and sipped mint leaf tea. When the interview started he wanted to be prepared.

51

Then Vesudeva looked at Emil and spoke. "Are you ready to begin?"

Nervously Emil replied, "Sure."

"Good," said Vesudeva. "However, before we start let us close our eyes and request guidance from the Unseen Forces. May they guide our efforts, so the readers might benefit."

Vesudeva closed his eyes and sat quietly, focusing inward. For some reason, this act of requesting guidance from something higher made Emil feel uneasy. He sat still and waited.

After a time Vesudeva opened his eyes, looked directly at Emil and offered, "Let's begin."

E: "Vesudeva, from your point of view, please tell the reader why spiritual learning is important. A skeptic might contend, 'I'm doing fine just the way I am. Why do I need something which cannot be seen or held?"

V: "Spiritual or higher knowledge is a part of you. In many it remains dormant or partially used. Unless awakened in the correct manner, this dimension, because it is energy, manifests as an undefined anxiety, yearning or emptiness. This emptiness and yearning, unless properly channeled and defined, can seek fulfillment in all types of destructive habits, lifestyles, and addictions. Because people feel empty or anxious inside- they seek to fill this emptiness with all manner of things. We call this emptiness the 'great yearning.' Without developing higher knowledge man is walking about using one leg, falling and going around in circles."

E: "Are you saying that many of the world's social ills and addictive problems arise from lack of higher spiritual development?"

V: "In part, yes, because people have not been taught to use this higher knowledge they are prone to making poor decisions. Some of these are in the form of lifestyle habits and addictions. Many choices relate to not using conscious energy in a positive and directed manner. These decisions emerge from an over concern with individual fears and then compensating these fears by doing selfish and destructive things to self and others."

E: "Can you explain what you mean by selfish actions that harm others?"

V: "Take, for example, a child who is poor and has no money. As this child grows, this child makes a decision never to be poor or without money again. The young child, now an adult, works tirelessly to amass material wealth neglecting other aspects of life. In the business world this person is relentless, often not caring about others and either directly or indirectly causes harm, trying to amass his personal fortune."

"In a balanced person there is present a concern for others as well as a concern for self. This concern for others often manifests in acts of charity and helping. The balanced person realizes concern for his neighbor is concern for self. We are all connected and the world will be a better place, if all are fed, clothed and housed."

"For you see selfishness or exaggerated concern for oneself helps create an imbalanced world or society. We all want a good world to live in and raise our family. It is in everyone's best interest to take care of their neighbor, because this person lives next door. If this neighbor becomes sick, might not the illness spread? Or if the neighbor has no food might not the neighbor's desperation turn into harmful action toward another?"

Vesudeva paused for a moment and could see Emil was thinking about what had been said. After a time Emil questioned further.

E: "If I understand you correctly, you are saying lack of higher development in some people leads to greed which can harm others. This sounds very simplistic. What about other influencing factors such as health, environment and inherent biologic capacity?"

V: "In recent years, science, economics, sociology and other learning systems have contributed much to our understanding these problems. This input is essential. Yet part of the puzzle remains unclear. From our perspective each person is born with inherent capacities and the potential to do many things. Unless all of these capacities are explored, refined, and properly used, the individual is incomplete and has not reached full potential. When groups of people are at full potential, using their higher knowledge along with other capacities, many people benefit. Similarly, as people are denied the opportunity to express the different parts of self, something is lacking. This void or emptiness, because capacity has not been used, leads toward much unhappiness and destructive action in the world."

"As it is with an individual, so it is with a town, city, or whole generation of people. One does not have to be very smart, intuitive or utilize higher capacity to know something is missing in our society. As a whole, we have become too materialistic and this exaggerated interest in self, to a large degree, has become destructive. Good people can make a good society."

E: "If one accepts your position, that higher development is essential to an individual's and society's existence, then, why isn't this more known and taught?"

V: "But it is! People are constantly advocating and asserting their position on all of this. Look about you. Some of the strongest forces in our society are the forces of organized religion and spiritual learning. Not making enough noise or energy spent advocating a position is not the problem. The problem as we view it is in 'sincerity' of action and 'world sickness.' Over time, some of the great religions sadly have become part of the problem. They no longer emphasize higher development and are overly concerned with their economic world."

E: "What do you mean? First you were saying spiritual development is essential, now you are saying some of the great religions are part of the problem. I am confused. Which is it?"

V: "Both things are true. Also, you are trying to work out this problem with your intellect and reasoning alone and are not using your higher or intuitive capacity. Your intellect reasons, how can both parts of this argument be true? Well, they are. Religion and spiritual learning can either be a hindrance to a person or a benefit. Remember, anything if used improperly can cause harm. Consider a cleaning agent like bleach. It is very good for certain clothes, but destructive to dark clothing.

"We are speaking about balanced development and correct application. Where higher knowledge is one element among many others. Also many paths, due to lack of 'sincerity' and 'world sickness' upon the part of their leaders, have turned faith into a means of control and manipulation.

"It is not our position to attack another's faith or religious belief. We are merely pointing out the universal tendency in human enterprises over time to lose effectiveness and initial intent."

E: "For people like myself, who may not be familiar with these terms, please define what you mean by 'sincerity' and 'world sickness.'

V: "From our point of view, 'world sickness' means that a person becomes overly concerned with the things of the world. This occurs to the point the individual loses sight of the importance of balanced living and the higher dimension.

  "The term 'sincerity' describes inner truthfulness. Often people are unaware when they mask one thing with another. For example, many times parents urge their children to do one thing or another. Is the thing being emphasized because of the child's well being or the need or fear of the parent? 'I do not want you to make the same mistakes as me.' While some of this advice may be good, a whole lot may not be. This lack of 'sincerity,' as we describe it, may be limiting for the child and not allow for free expression."

E: "OK. How do these terms apply to paths, their leadership and organized religious enterprises?"

V: "In order for a path to flourish and have a visible presence in the world, some believe more buildings, books, schools, and training programs are better. It is a human trait to believe, 'the bigger the better,' yet this statement is not true for everything all the time.

  "Sometimes spiritual enterprises get overly concerned with worldly activity to the point, the higher balance is disrupted. Many times people who are advocating certain actions are not consciously aware a particular activity is based upon greed or something they personally want. There is such a thing as spiritual greed. These people assert, 'I want my faith to do the best it can for others and I know this action is the best way.'

"These are common mistakes. Often made in the name of doing good for others."

ᔥ   ᔥ

Let us play a game and suppose you could be anything you desire. Pick someone or something and pretend you are that person or thing for a moment. Concentrate and imagine yourself being whatever you like.

Now consider how far from the truth this really was. For an instant, a part of you was someone or something else. For that moment you consciously changed a part of your reality.

Now take this technique of changing your consciousness and use it for a Higher Purpose.

ᔥ

In the journey there comes a point when words and desires are no longer important. That is, there is no emotional attachment to them. All that is important is the Source. Desire for everything else has been removed.

It is at this point the traveler arrives and the Source is within sight. However for most this is not a static condition. The traveler fluctuates between this state and others. The degree of fluctuation is in proportion to the traveler's position on the path and the work he/she is required to do.

ᔥ

Feeling spiritual is not the same thing as being spiritual. Most people confuse emotional states with spiritual ones; remaining satisfied with fool's gold.

ᔥ

The canvas is the world: you are the artist.
Pick up the brush and create your own life.

10

A Matter of Effect

On one level people want simple answers and to be told what to do. On another, they want freedom to choose and make their own decisions. People have the capacity to do both: make their own choices as well as accept direction from others. Discord sets in when the guidance from others or authority does not fit what the individual wants or feels is right for them. In this case, the individual is in conflict and looks for something else.

Most people are taught a philosophy of 'right and wrong.' At an early age, aspects of this protective mechanism are applied to daily life and are part of social and religious training. For example, if you do not get up on time and arrive timely at school this is bad. As an adult, being late will eventually result in loss of job.

From a higher perspective, looking at daily events: travelers are taught to take a more longitudinal and holistic view of the effect of specific actions. In real life, often it is not a simple matter of an action being 'right or wrong.' Actions are complex and involve others, having both a collective and individual effect. Before making many decisions, it is wise to consider the long term and multi-level effect.

As an example, how about the common situation where your beloved asks- do you think I have put on a few pounds? Does this dress/suit make me look fat? Sometimes telling the truth can be unnecessarily hurtful; particularly if the individual has been struggling with their weight. In most situations, we are free to pick and choose how to respond.

Further when viewing the effect of personal action, it is impossible to know all the variables involved; particularly over a long period of time and actions that affect countless others. However, for the spiritual traveler, it is possible to know some of this and begin any decision making process by asking the question: will this action bring me closer or distance me from my higher destiny?

The answer to this question may be thought out as well as perceived. First, we rationally consider and list the effects using what we term our common sense. Next, we use our intuition, requesting if the action will bring us closer or distance us from our higher self. Perception is intuitive knowledge that emerges from our collective consciousness. By turning inward, the traveler unlocks this holistic 'gut' awareness and uses this answer along with their rational thought to arrive at an action.

At an early age, it is important to learn about the difference between right and wrong. It is important to learn some things are good for us and some things are not. Yet, spiritual teaching must go deeper, illustrating and considering the aspect of longitudinal effect and destiny. While one piece of chocolate may be tasty and even nutritious, twenty is not; particularly, if we are diabetic or prone to dental problems.

Most spiritual training programs teach the traveler to pray, or turn inward in some fashion or another before taking an important action. Within each person, there is an inner voice or capacity to know if an action will bring us closer to our own higher self and the higher destiny of the universe. Most people have forgotten to develop and listen to their own inner voice and have relied upon others to teach them about right and wrong.

This original social, moral and religious teaching, about what is useful in life, was intended as a beginning; and travelers, as they matured, were to be instructed on how to make their own more complex, intuitive decisions. For many, this has been omitted from their training and they continue to rely upon limited and simplistic societal learning constructs, many of which have been tied to a 'fear & reward' system. In a sense, for these travelers, their thoughts on certain subjects have become fixed, often engineered by others.

ℴ   ℴ

E mil and Vesudeva were on a break from their question and answer session. In the woods adjacent to the hut, they were picking wild raspberries for lunch. As Vesudeva picked from the small bush next to Emil, Vesudeva inquired, "Have you ever considered the difference between these wild fruit and yourself?"

Emil, a little puzzled, replied, "Vesudeva, are you speaking with me or formulating a question aloud?"

"No, I'm not talking to myself. Let me restate and add to the question. What is the difference between this wild fruit and you? Also, how are you both similar?"

Emil stopped picking. His back was sore from bending over. He stood up and looked directly at Vesudeva. Emil saw that Vesudeva was serious. He was awaiting an answer. This was not an idle question and Emil anxiously thought about his reply, wishing not to offend. "Well, let me answer the second part of the question first. This seems easiest. These raspberries and I are the same in that we are both creations of the Source and in this respect serve a function."

"Very good," Vesudeva replied. "Now, what are the differences?"

"H'mm. Let me see. First, I am more complex and have

60

many things to consider. Also, a raspberry is a fruit and I am a man. As a fruit, its function is to be eaten. My function as a man is multi-level and more complex. How's that for an answer? Vesudeva smiled, then replied, "Your answer is a good beginning with fine elements to it. However, in stating you are complex you need to further consider what this actually means. From our perspective, what separates man from others is free will and levels of consciousness. All creatures have complexity and awareness. What separates man is free will and how these choices through individual awareness influence the capacity to create reality. Your effect upon your world and others, in part is up to you."

"What do you mean? I'm not certain that I follow what you are saying."

Vesudeva put down the bowl of raspberries, sat on the forest floor and motioned for Emil to sit beside him. Vesudeva closed his eyes for a moment, focused inward and concentrated.

"All creatures have differing levels of consciousness and awareness. Similarly, all creatures serve multi-level functions. Man because of his uniqueness has been created with the capacity to help influence his own world and reality. Through higher consciousness and thought man becomes a creator. This fruit has an awareness of its world and its connection to the Source. Yet in comparison to man's role and consciousness, it is very limited."

Emil spoke, "I'm not sure I fully understand how thoughts are related to creation of reality? Please further explain this idea."

"Man is a being of conscious energy. Daily, this energy is directed to help keep the body alive, monitoring physical and emotional systems and creating mind awareness. On many levels, this awareness is physical, mental and spiritual. In fact it originates on a deep inner level that we have come to term 'spiritual' and is directed out through our physical bodies."

"Thought is energy which can be projected out into the universe. This energy has both the function and capacity to interact and influence other people and unseen elements. This world about us is filled with all types of invisible energy."

"Let me give a practical example. It is common knowledge that in order for a man to accomplish a task, he must first conceive the task as a possibility. He must want to accomplish it. And the more that the man believes in this idea and works toward its fulfillment, the greater chance that the idea will be accomplished."

"In this aspect of using conscious energy- man is the creator. Like the Source is the Creator. A person who constantly thinks or believes negative things, in part causes these things to occur."

By this time, Emil was growing confused. This highly technical discussion about energy was giving him a headache and he was uncertain how it applied to him. Growing anxious, Emil started to nibble on the wild raspberries.

Chuckling to himself, Vesudeva saw that he lost his student, stood and began walking back to the hut. Growing more anxious, Emil stood and followed. All the while wondering how this discussion concerning thought as energy and creative force was related to anything.

෨

Seated at the outdoor table, sipping tea, Vesudeva continued. "It is not important for you to understand everything I am saying. My words will affect you on different levels and deep within yourself there is a center that I am directing this energy toward. Over time, as the Source Wills, you will perceive the effects."

"Now, thoughts, ideas, and desires all have conscious energy that are very powerful. Many people understand this and have used ideas, ideologies and even religious teaching to influence action. Much of what you have been taught about the world has been filtered through other people's awareness. Because of the individual nature of consciousness, some of these ideas and teachings are presented in a partially distorted or limited form.

"Much of what we teach our students is to perceive reality directly, free of other's distortions and influences. In order to do this, you must learn to push aside for a time your ideas about the world, yourself and religion. Much of this awareness has been engineered into you and is not completely accurate. By temporarily suspending preconceived notions and ordinary thought, you can learn to experience what there is in yourself and the world, free of these unreal ideas and accompanying emotions.

"A student who is mature has learned to master his own consciousness, ideas and emotions. Do you understand?" Emil moved his head up and down, as if he understood. But he really wasn't getting all of this. He desperately wanted to go back to the interview format, where he asked the questions and was in control.

ഇ   ഇ

Humanity is conscious energy
Burning like sunlight.
By reflecting the Light into this world
Humanity neutralizes personal spiritual darkness.

Embrace your own inner beliefs
And then travel beyond them.
Embrace higher knowledge
And as the Source Wills
You will become a sun unto yourself:
Knowing right from wrong,
Dissipating your own lower needs and desires.

ഇ

What some call religious training and tradition:
Often is based upon historical and no longer accurate,
Incomplete information; also, in some presentations
There is tendency to misapply traditional exercises to modern culture;
Further, many sacred books include
Selective reportage by believers and historians;
With altered teachings to control desired behaviors
Which were insisted upon by the ruling entity.

Remember many cherished religious traditions and behaviors
no longer serve any real or spiritual function.
However, they do increase people's feelings of comfort/tradition
And need to be viewed within this emotional framework.

ဆ

— 11 —

Repetition & Formula

One of the characteristics of the way our mind works is to create order, categorize and use repetition to help establish a sense of familiarity. Additionally, this tendency toward repetition is one of the aspects of the physical universe. Repetition exists within nature and helps form and create our world view. This tendency serves a number of important functions and it would be simplistic, although partially true, to say it is a reaction against the chaos in the universe and our own eventual physical death.

The ancients recognized great cycles within the universe and natural world; aligning aspects of their lives around these naturally occurring patterns. For example, in parts of the world there are four seasons, 24 hours in a day, 12 months in a year and three meals, daily. The term of pregnancy is considered nine months and each person is born, lives and dies. These natural cycles with their repetitious patterns bring order to our lives and help form the way we look at life. Sometimes we react strongly when events do not adhere and coincide with expected patterns.

Consider the construct of time or 24 hours in a day. A song calls out the lyrics, "Does anyone really know what time it is?" When did humans first begin keeping time? When did time actually start? For dolphins swimming beneath the ocean surface is it really 12 o'clock and time for lunch? If we travel to a far away planet and meet little green people; will they all be wearing Mickey Mouse watches and waiting until 7 pm to watch their favorite show on the Disney Channel? Probably not.

Some might assert, man created the concept of time based upon certain naturally occurring patterns in the universe and this concept is useful in many ways. However, like all things this construct can be over worked and lose effectiveness. For example, consider the common situation of an office worker with a private refrigerator who is hungry at 11:30 a.m. and it is not time for lunch. That is, it is not 12:00 p.m. and he walks around hungry for 30 minutes until it is time to eat from his own brown bag lunch. At 11:30 a.m., what is stopping this fellow from having a bite of his own sandwich? An ingrained adherence to a construct or pattern. Traditional office convention states it is not lunch time and it is too early to eat. But this is not a constructive use of the concept of time – at least with regard to this person's biological need for food.

For the spiritual traveler, it is important to recognize the effect of repetition upon higher studies. Repetition can be both useful and limiting. Consider the possibility that some religions use historical and traditional prayers, exercises and formulas that have for many followers outlived their inner vibrancy. In contrast, other frameworks state that in order for a teaching to be vibrant and alive it must be updated from time to time. Circumstances and people vary. Ideas, customs and formulas that were created for one culture do not easily translate to another time and place. Yet, due to an overriding need for tradition and repetition, worn out methods remain in use, and are not supplemented with newer material. Fortunately, each person has an inner voice that helps them discern when this may be occurring. Unfortunately, many do not learn to trust their own inner wisdom; bound to worn traditions that lack personal meaning and inner usefulness.

Numerous traditions operate within the framework of a living teacher who updates the teaching for each student, time and place. Within this structure, the world is never without exemplars and their function in part is to be living proof of the tradition's viability. Older formulas, prayers and instructions are superseded and the present way is offered.

In the field of spiritual studies, as in any endeavor, the traveler must be an educated consumer. False and authentic teachers exist. To make matters more complicated, often false teachers do not realize they are using worn out or incomplete methods. Often these teachers present specific formulas, instruction and constructs in the same way for years and for each individual student.

For example, follow 10 Steps to Enlightenment. Say this prayer 5 times a day and you will reach the journey's end. While each of these learning exercises may have inner usefulness, for a time, they are not complete systems. In an authentic school, repetition is used for specific purposes and is not a dominant aspect of the teaching and each student is given an individual course of study that is monitored by the teacher.

In higher learning, repetition and our need for comfort and formula can be a limiting factor; particularly if this is all we are taught.

ဢ   ဢ

Nervously, Emil was reviewing his notes and written questions, wanting to return to the structured format. Vesudeva was quiet and waited patiently, having sensed Emil's need to return to more familiar ground. Finally, Emil got up enough nerve and resumed asking questions.

E: "Vesudeva, in this age many people are searching for something higher. This search is all around us and this interest is the reason for the newspaper series. What then is the core of your teaching? If the traveler were to focus on one aspect or rule what would that be?"

V: "My teaching is both simple and complex. It is the perennial teaching: to Love the Source with all your heart and soul. Everything the traveler needs is contained in this statement."

E: "For those travelers who may be just starting out, how does one learn to Love the Source?"

V: "Love is something that is not taught. It either is or is not. Because of early experiences or conditions in the world, many have been hurt and have turned away. "Within each traveler there is a part that is continually unified with the Source. The task of the traveler is to awaken and recognize this part of himself."

E: "How does the traveler do this?"

V: "By studying in the presence of a teacher."

E: "And if a teacher is not available, what does the traveler do?"

V: Smiling Vesudeva continued, "The teachers are always present. In our classroom, there is no time and space and the teaching is perennially projected and then perceived by that part of the traveler that some people term their subconscious. The teaching is projected on an inner level. Even when one is physically in the presence of the teacher, the real, inner teaching is on another level of awareness. Also much of the teaching takes place in the evening when the traveler is sleeping."

E: Surprised and not fully understanding what Vesudeva was saying, Emil sputtered, "Do you actually believe readers will understand and accept learning can and does take place while you are sleeping?"

V: Laughing Vesudeva replied, "What? You don't believe this? My friend, you have not even kept up-to-date with your own learning sciences. A while ago, it was proven people could learn a new language while they slept. By playing a tape recording of words in both languages, native and new, language students could learn to speak different words and phrases. Also, psychologists have trained their patients to wake up and record dreams, then go back to sleep. Working from these notes, over the next days, patients could examine and learn from inner processes through dream analysis."

"Remember: just because you do not see something it does not mean it does not exist."

E: Emil paused and thought for a few moments about what Vesudeva was saying. Not getting it all, he returned to his notes and inquired. "From your perspective, tell us why man comes to this world? For what reason?"

V: "Once again, what I offer is not my philosophy or idea. It is an eternal truth as revealed through the Teaching. This is the timeless, inner reality. This answer has been hidden, because people rejected and at certain times killed those who offered it."

"Man enters the earth phase of being for many, many reasons. Chief among these reasons is to learn and grow closer to the Source. The earth phase is a very special place and multi-level experience. Within this world, man has the capacity to further advance: as creator of his own reality and universe. We all have an aspect of the Source within and this is the magical element that allows us to create reality.

"Upon entering, man brings with him talents, capacities and needs that help generate a Life Plan. This plan is both personal and universal. It is partially known and partially hidden from the traveler. Everyone has a plan so they can learn and draw closer. This plan, combined with our innate skills, helps to propel man through his day to day life toward his higher destiny. Each person knows, on some level, what they like and wish to become. As they go along, the traveler participates in the building and planning of life through both mundane and spiritual activities. Other forces help direct and steer the outcome toward its unique expression."

"As they go through life, most people forget their purpose, and must apply directed effort to remember where they came from and where they are going. This is where the Teaching can be most helpful. It enables the traveler to remember and reconnect with their higher capacity and individual plan."

"Because the physical body, on one level, is a pleasure machine and tied to the sensual, many get lost in this physical reality. The physical exists in part as a catalyst to enable the fuller expression of the spiritual. It is the friction between the two which makes the great wheel of life turn."

"As previously indicated, one of the characteristics of the physical universe is repetition. Natural laws keep the physical universe in balance. The inner capacity of man, in part, exists to temporarily shatter this repetition and formula. It is a framework to allow something else to occur. Do you follow?"

E: "No. Not really."

V: "Let me come at this another way. In most spiritual learning structures, prayer and exercises are given that provide a basis from which something else might happen. By saying a prayer, focusing and turning inward, the physical capacities are stilled so that the inner awareness might come forward. That is the inner aspect to formulary prayer. This is the same principle I am describing here. The only difference is I am not describing what to you would be a traditional church and priest/parishioner relationship.

The teacher exists in the main, to show this inner capacity to the student and when this part has matured, the teacher is no longer needed. Then the traveler proceeds on their own."

E: "This sounds like a difficult thing to grasp and learn."

V: "Fear not. It is a natural process and is as familiar as breathing air. Once the traveler realizes this is just another aspect of self and has always been present, the traveler seeks to express him or herself in this area as well."

"Spiritual expression, while the center of life, is one aspect to the overall design. People miss the point if they believe that to be a spiritual person one must continually deny other aspects of life. All of our capacities and needs are part of the journey."

E: "If this is so, why do some run off and become hermits avoiding the world?"

V: "Initially, this experience of solitude was presented as a type of learning or exercise. After the lessons were learned, the student was meant to go on with other aspects of life. That is why in many accounts; this experience was for a fixed period. Learning was to occur that would be useful in the world.

"Some became confused and turned a learning experience into a lifestyle. But, higher learning exists to make for a fuller life and better world for everyone. How would the affairs of the world continue if everyone ran off into a cave to contemplate their navel? Someone has to work the rivers, fields and have the babies. Yes, we all must set aside a period of quiet time for contemplation, solitude and inner learning. However, we are also to participate in the world. Do you see?"

E: "Does this mean that all those who have gone to spiritual learning centers apart from the world are incorrect?"

V: "I do not know other people's destinies and what is in their hearts. If someone chooses to live a life apart, not marry and deny themselves certain things, so they can draw closer to the Source that is between them and the Source.

"The original way, the perennial way is that this is not required. We are complex beings, have many levels and are to enjoy the world fully expressing who we are. On an inner level man knows what is constructive and what is destructive. He has an innate sense to all of this."

E: "If man has an inner sense concerning what is destructive, why is there so much suffering in the world?"

V: "Man is the origin of much of his own suffering and pain, giving the Source far too much credit concerning this. Man creates the wars. Man is full of greed; leaving many homeless and hungry. If allocated differently, the world has enough resources to feed the hungry, clothe the poor and care for the sick. Man chooses to do other things, blaming others and the Source.

"Remember, in many ways, man creates his own reality, world and destiny. This is free will."

E: "Do you mean there is no evil or devil?"

V: "Man is creator of his own universe and collectively humanity creates a larger reality and world.

"In our view evil is that which distances you from the Source. It is an action or thought which blocks the higher potential from coming forward. Most people are born with an inner sense of right and wrong."

E: Persisting, Emil inquired again, "Is there no devil?"

V: "All action and thought is energy in the form of vibrations. That which is destructive to man has an energy and vibration. This energy blocks the higher from coming forward. This negative energy, many term evil. It has a very strong presence and reality.

"For the most part, the devil that is portrayed in the media, with horns and tail is a product of collective imagination. A reality exists but not like this.

"Remember, all the traveler needs to vanquish evil is the Holy Name."

          ॐ   ॐ

People have both heaven and hell within their heart.
We are all creators of a vast universe- ourselves-
And must continuously remember to choose higher.

     ॐ

Often people are reluctant and fearful
About acting in their own best interest.
Even when the negative pattern
Has been repeated hundreds of times.
This is the universal tendency toward repetition
Pulling against a new opportunity.

     ॐ

Much of human activity can be explained
Through observing our personal excitement need.
Daily we seek stimulation and attention.
These two basic needs drive us in all kinds of directions.

Many seek a spiritual path that will be both stimulating and exciting;
Forgetting they should be looking for a path- that works.

ॐ

Each person's consciousness is a series of repeating patterns which are like the rooms of a fine house. Each room is decorated with paint, curtains, furniture and other pieces. While these adornments reflect the owner's individuality, the room is a bedroom, dining room or kitchen. It has a function which combines with the others to make up the house.

Often we become jailors, content to live our lives in these rooms only. We never consider there may be another world beyond these walls. That is why each house has a door. The wise learn to use it.

ॐ

How does one learn? We are taught by parents, by school, by religion and by society. This is how we learn to make choices. We choose based upon what we are taught to see.

How do we break free of this patterned thought and existence? Why do we want freedom?

Foolish one- it is our destiny to learn to see beyond the world of appearances. There is a yearning within that cannot be stilled- until the bird of the soul soars free.

ॐ

— 12 —

The Work

For the spiritual traveler, the concept of work is multi-level and as one travels further along the path, takes on added dimension. From a spiritual perspective, each moment, experience and interchange has both a fixed and unlimited potential. Additionally, this potential is personal and collective; both tied to the moment, and to a higher design.

As example, compare the similarities between the work of a young child and an elected official. The young child experiences and learns from each moment. In time, these experiences come together to form the pattern of an emerging personality and life. While the elected official works to meet the needs of a constituency, both now and in the future; he or she also strives to meet personal and family needs.

When viewing the concept of work, how are the needs of a young child and politician related to the work of a spiritual master? One master has offered, "The path, or work is none other than in human service." How does this ideal relate to practical, daily life and ultimate progress along a path?

The work of a young child is to grow, learn and experience. By living in the moment and being herself, in time she learns skills, attitudes and emotional responses that will be of use throughout her life. This period is characterized by an emphasis upon exploring, learning and experiencing the different aspects of self and the world. Each impact is important and lays the framework for future learning. One might say, in this respect her life is similar to that of a politician who uses past and present experience to do the work of the moment and plan for the future. This is both on a personal and vocational level. Each person is a combination of past learning, and uses this learning to participate in their present experience.

The orientation of the spiritual traveler is that in each moment there is a crisis. For each moment has a higher potential with both fixed and transcendent outcomes. In each moment, we have the choice for personal selfishness or service to our higher self and the universe. Reaching higher is accomplished by attaching individual will to a higher design. On one level, while we are eating our breakfast to gain nutrition; if this is dedicated to something higher- this activity aligns with the spiritual dimension. By shifting focus we shift intention- from self to the higher good.

When this orientation, service to humanity is used in daily life, each action takes on a higher vibration. This energy and vibration -through shift in intention- is different. By stilling individual need and turning over individual desire; we become 'transparent' and another, higher will has the potential to operate.

For the traveler, each moment is filled with the opportunity to learn, enjoy and serve. This is accomplished by focusing on the task at hand, doing the best we can and shifting intention from self to the higher. In each opportunity, inquire, who are we serving by performing this action or thinking these thoughts?

Remember. Align action and intention with your higher destiny and the higher, emerging destiny of the universe. In this way, we make each moment a working prayer.

ဢ   ဢ

Nestor started the return voyage back to the ferryman's hut. On this run, no passengers, only five large reed baskets filled with the uncommon spices of qalb, ruh, sirr, khafil and ikfa; that a merchant arranged to pickup on the other side. This pickup would be in two days and during this time the baskets were to be stored in the shade, dockside. These black, green, white, yellow and light red enhancements, when mixed together in the correct amount and sprinkled on food, produced a tasty life enhancing flavor.

Usually the ferryman did not engage in either storage or guarding cargo, but this opportunity could not be ignored. What Nestor learned in the world of commerce was that for the right price, just about anything was possible. People were capable of remarkable things, in a very short period, provided the motivation or money was right.

In the world of spiritual studies the motivation was generated by a different value system. Will the action bring you closer or distance you from the Beloved? To answer life's questions, another capacity had to be awakened and used. This was spiritual sight or the inner dimension Vesudeva worked with, asserting there was nothing magical or mysterious about all of this. This capacity was an extension of conscious awareness that was within everyone.

As Nestor worked the oar, he guided the raft across the deep waters. Feeling the warm midday sun across his back and flowing with the motion of the river and universe, Nestor offered up a silent prayer.

ဢ

E: "Are you saying, there is no such thing as evil or the devil?"

V: "On one level, from our perspective, everything is a learning experience. All action and reaction has the potential to teach the traveler something. We instruct travelers to examine events, actions, and feelings so the lesson may be harvested and life more fully understood. By learning to see the design or structure in life events: the traveler may learn to see another level. Beyond the outward manifestation of worldly events, the spiritual dimension is operating."

E: But . . . you still have not answered the question. Is there evil or a devil?"

V: "In our view, man is both creator and devil. Constructing wonderful things and destroying others. If it pleases you, or makes you content, to think of the universe in this way, then embrace this view. Understand that our view is different and is about vibrations, energy, learning and potentiality.

"Let us take an example. War. Everyone would agree this is a terrible event; with many lives, resources, and countries being destroyed or harmed. Yet there are often remarkable outgrowths of this damaging experience. Once, after a large war that involved the great countries of the world, many of the soldiers who had been in combat were exhibiting nervous disorders, extreme fear and depression. Countless numbers, as a result of their war experience, could no longer function in the world. To help remedy this problem, scientists and physicians worked on and developed a new class of psychiatric medicines to help heal these soldiers. In time, these medicines were made available to the general population and stimulated the creation of countless others, thereby helping many others over the years."

"Here is another example that occurred centuries ago as a result of a 'Holy War.' Many fine warriors left their country to free 'The Holy City,' from those they considered non-believers; who were inferior to themselves and agents of the devil. In the fighting that ensued, many fine men lost their lives on both sides. For you see, both sides believed they were correct, fighting for their God.

"In time, the cultural exchange which occurred as a secondary consequence to the fighting led to positive things. There was an exchange of art, ideas, and trade routes were expanded to make available different resources to both sides. Also, some thoughtful men and women began to wonder how both sides could be correct and believe this action was for their God."

"In this particular war, over time it became clear that the selfish interests of some stood in the way of the many. Why this was termed a 'Holy War' who can say? Clearly it was about something else: land, gold, trade routes and power."

80

E: "In all of this you raise a very interesting point. Typically disagreements persist and wars are fought because both sides believe they are correct. How can this be overcome?"

V: "Because we are trained at a young age to believe there is a right and a wrong way; we never examine the possibility there may be a third way or a dozen other ways. And all of these ways or paths are bound in the energy of belief. Belief is a very powerful ingredient. For many things, not all: it is the operative aspect. Tied to the energy of belief is the potential for actualization. Many people are successful in an endeavor, simply because they believe and the energy that comes about through belief, increases potential. If they did not believe, they would have given-up; belief being a catalyst or spring board."

E: "Well then, is it possible for two seemingly opposite things to be true at the same time?"

V: Laughing. Vesudeva replied, "Have you never been in love? One day you are enamored with a beautiful woman and the next because of a disagreement you hate her. One day love. The next hate. Well. Which one is it?

"The universal essence expresses itself in many forms including opposites. There are many worlds and dimensions that are hidden, yet they exist. Is it possible for more than one thing to be true at the same time? Of course it is.

'Looking at the earth, from the moon, this world with all its divergent aspects is one creation.' This was said by one of the great teachers of our path. Another saying, 'the sun is always shining, even in the night. Just because you do not see a thing, it does not mean it ceases to exist.'

E: "With all due respect, you have many fine sayings and your arguments appear sound, but how can these convince the skeptic what you say is true? These are just words and skeptics have their own words and arguments. What is the point of all this fencing with words?"

V: "We do not ask that anyone accept our point of view. What we offer is an alternative view that has existed since the beginning. What we suggest, if you are a serious student; is to consider this view as a working framework, a hypothesis, until your own experience proves or disproves it."

"If you automatically reject something because it does not fit your belief system, you deny yourself the opportunity to fully examine an alternate view. How else does one move forward in their beliefs? You must be neutral in this thing. Seeking only to view what is there, not what you or others say is there or believe is present."

"In the science that we practice, the traveler is given their own experience as a measuring stick. This experience is always in a form that is both universal and highly personal. As the Source Wills, the traveler experiences this reality and other realities."

E: "Why should anyone believe any of this?"

V: "They should not believe anything and examine these statements and their validity on their own, seeking personal proof. However, like any learning system the traveler will advance more quickly by following the guidance of a skilled teacher."

₞   ₞

There is a plan for humanity.
We are all evolving upward;
Collectively humanity is reaching toward
Full conscious awareness; and using this awareness
To partner in the Higher Design.

One day, this dream will become reality.
Until then- journey inward.
Say the prayer of submission
And embrace your higher self through the Light.
In this experience, you will be assisted
By the Unseen Forces- who help bring forward the Plan.

₞

Once you have learned that which you came here to learn;
That is the first step. Next you must put this knowledge to work.
The wise are those who serve out of love;
And make their life's work an extension of the Source.

— 13 —

Added Responsibility

Early on in the exchange between student and teacher, it is stressed that spiritual learning is in addition to the responsibilities of ordinary life. Daily, each traveler is made aware that the point of higher knowledge is to produce someone 'who is part of the world but not of the world.' The traveler must have a job, join in the daily commerce, have family and friends; yet a part must remain sacred, separate and detached. What is necessary for complete development is an 'ordinary person' who burns for something higher. This spiritual burning must be in correct balance with other personality and social factors.

Consequently the traveler is not free from daily responsibility or the trials that befall all of humanity: sickness and loss of loved ones. These experiences are part of life and essential to our human experience. Because of a certain inner orientation: the traveler has an additional way to look at these often troubling aspects of daily life. Often this view is integrating and loving and provides a holistic and more accepting framework.

ဢ

We achieve some of our greatest successes when we overcome problems.

ဢ

Tears of laughter and sorrow are one; springing from the great reservoir of hope. Both of these tears are a blessing; uniting us in the Beloved's Love.

Drink deeply from this water. It is the spring of life and will carry us through the many worlds.

සෝ

The climb is steep and the road is long. There are many dangers and many joys. Through the journey- what is required is a certain attitude or view that seeks the connecting and liberating factor.

If you are seeking a road that is filled with excitement, strange clothing and exotic friends- this is not the road for you. If you seek the ordinary through which the extra-ordinary manifests: then this road might be for you. Yet are you worthy and capable of the climb?

This is the question that you must ask your heart. The lovers have only one reply.

සෝ

Remember, the world has enough hermits and those who wish to run from life. What is required is someone who jumps into the river and saves themselves. In the process, the swimmer is able to pull others from the dangerous currents.

Are you a swimmer? Can you over come the dangerous water? Only by the help and grace of those who have gone before. Heed their example. Familiarize yourself with their teachings.

සෝ   සෝ

By now Nestor was halfway across the river and noticed up ahead, four boatloads of fisherman gliding on the current. In each boat, Nestor observed two or three men standing with spears in hand. Usually spear fishing was best in the shallows and as Nestor continued to work the oar and move steadily forward, he wondered about that?

Drawing closer to the fisherman, Nestor called to the lead boat, "Ho! What are you going for?"

Somewhat startled, because all eyes had been fixed upon the water, one of the older fishermen called, "Ho! Friend. Be careful. Something very big and dangerous has entered these waters. This morning, upriver we have lost one of our boats with two men aboard."

Nestor began to get an unsettled feeling in his stomach. He had heard stories about rogue crocodiles and very large anacondas, but in these deep waters? Somehow this did not fit the pattern. As he continued on Nestor called, "Is it safe to work these waters?"

One of the other fishermen replied, "We do not know? But if you could stay off the river for a time that might be wise."

"Thanks," Nestor called back and he began to scan the river even faster. Unsure what he was searching for, Nestor wanted to remain alert to every possible danger.

~

Emil studied Vesudeva's replies to the various questions and wondered how this philosophy applied to his own and the lives of the newspaper readers? As Vesudeva heated their lunch of fish and vegetable stew, Emil reread the different responses. He wondered, where next to take the interview? To Emil, this philosophy or doctrine seemed sugary and almost too good to be true. "Love the Source with all your heart and soul." "Seek to make your life an hour of service." Did anyone actually believe this and, in fact, make the Light the center of their life? When Nestor returned, he was due back before lunch; Emil would ask Nestor about this. For now, Emil selected additional questions from those he had prepared.

~

V: "When the traveler enters upon our path, religious duties and spiritual learning become an extension of a higher level of consciousness. They emerge from a growing inner awareness that has been kindled by the Light of Eternity. Our followers are expected to enter into the main stream of life, participate in the world as any ordinary citizen and through purposeful effort help make the world a better place. Higher consciousness is added so it might help others in their daily life. Ours is the original human development system. The goal being through inner development, actualize each person as a unique entity who strives for individual excellence."

E: "In our time, there are many different paths, religions and human development programs that make similar claims. 'Follow us. We will make you into a more complete version of yourself.' Why should anyone accept what you say as the 'real' truth?"

V: "In our discussion, as I have indicated we do not exist to convince either you or your readers of anything. We are not in the business of recruiting students or followers. Follow whoever you like. It matters not to us.

"People are attracted to us like bees to a fragrant flower. Students perceive inwardly a compatibility with our expression of the timeless, then, make application to learn. We do not take out advertisements or send representatives into the market place to call students with program announcements. Enrollment is accomplished inwardly. Before joining, our students must be at a certain level of maturity. Within their own community, they must have reached a degree of balance, then, perceive the inner call. Over time, we add the missing ingredient so their lives might be more complete and tuned to a higher reality."

As Nestor distanced himself from the fishermen he began to feel uneasy, and was sweating more than usual. Suddenly, the hair on the back of his neck stood-up. His head and stomach ached. Instinctively, he stopped rowing the rear paddle and kept the raft still.

Suddenly, Nestor heard a loud 'thud' on the underside of the raft. It felt as if the raft hit and bounced off something very large. Like a submerged tree. Nestor knew the water was too deep for a tree to affect the raft this way and held his breath. Then, before he could scan the river to see what caused the problem, Nestor and the raft were lifted out of the water and tilted on its side. As Nestor was suspended in air momentarily beneath the raft, he heard a terrible, loud and frightening - "RRROOOAAARRR."

Hitting the water, a few feet from the now capsized raft, Nestor called out to the fishermen, "Help! Help me!" And as the baskets of spice mixed with the river, the waters turned deep shades of black, green, white, yellow and red-orange.

Without warning, Nestor felt a ripping and tearing in his right leg just below the knee. And as Nestor screamed again for help, he was pulled down below the surface far into the cold, dark water.

By now, frantically, the fishermen were speeding toward the capsized raft, calling loudly, "Hold on! Hold on! We are coming."

ॐ

Without a word Vesudeva stopped speaking. He closed his eyes, concentrated and sat silently. Emil did not know what to make of this action. One moment Vesudeva was discussing a point about multilevel responsibility, then, he stopped, closed his eyes and remained quiet. Emil wondered what he should do. He felt awkward. Should he leave or sit. Emil decided to wait.

After a time, Vesudeva opened his eyes, looked sadly at Emil and whispered, "Sometimes in life it is difficult to understand why things happen, but we must trust, be patient and continue."

Emil was shaken by the tone of deep sadness expressed in Vesudeva's words. Emil wondered what Vesudeva learned during those silent moments. Usually Vesudeva's eyes sparkled with happiness, energy and Light. Now it seemed as if the Light had gone out replaced by shadows. Emil was frightened and sat perfectly still unable to move.

Without further explanation, Vesudeva continued with the lesson.

V: "Man enters into the earth phase, taking on a physical body so that he can learn and more fully experience the Source. Here because of the sharp contrast between the physical and spiritual, the degree to which learning can occur is increased.

"The completed person, one whose hidden centers have all been activated, has the capacity to act in accord with the Divine Will. Through this activation of spiritual centers, which in some can be accomplished in a moment and others across lifetimes; the individual is aligned with the Source and in this realm become its representative.

"After this activation, real or more serious service to humanity is possible. Each person is a unique expression of the Source and travels across the many realms, living different lives expressing who they are. This life, this world, is one stop along the road back to the Source. We are all eternal rays of light that have been sent out into the universe, to learn, love, serve and express who we are in relation to the Source and make our way back home."

80

Then, Vesudeva was interrupted by a series of noises. From where Emil was seated he saw a group of fishermen mooring their boats to the ferryman's dock. Towing behind what was left of the raft, the fishermen excitedly called out, "Vesudeva! Vesudeva! Come, quickly, we have a terrible thing to tell you."

Startled by the fishermen's news, Emil began to grow even more frightened. Emil wondered, "Where was Nestor? Has Nestor been injured?"

Quickly, Emil understood, "Earlier when Vesudeva grew sad, he had seen this problem. Where was Nestor?"

ဆ   ဆ

This path is the original human development system.
It exists in part to bring about human excellence.

This path is not for everyone. It is for the courageous
And those who burn with love.

ဆ

Once there was a man who traveled all the highways in search of Truth. He stopped at every town and inquired. Sometimes the answers he received appeared to be useful and at other times they did not. Sometimes the advice he received was targeted at his worldly life: get a job, marry, have children. Or don't work, live in a monastery and become a recluse.

Somehow these pieces of advice did not satisfy, so, he kept on searching. One day, as luck would have it, he encountered a wise man who said: the answer lies within. So for years, this traveler with the help of the wise one examined the inner world and came to see these experiences and knowledge as part of the answer.

Slowly he realized: what good is spiritual knowledge if it is not used in the world? So he settled down, found a job, married and raised a family. As he worked, celebrated and worried, he came to see that a truly spiritual life is a life that serves others and is guided by the Unseen Forces. And according to design, he found real knowledge

88

and used this knowledge in the way it was intended.

80

— 14 —

Excitement, Stimulation & Attention

Part of daily life is the search for mental and physical stimulation, excitement and personal attention. These are very strong psychological/sociological needs and must be filled or we develop an inner longing and emptiness. Often, in a search for higher knowledge, this psychological emptiness or longing gets confused with the higher emptiness.

In part, our body and mind are built for pleasure and active living. When the correct amount of physical and mental stimulation is not present: the balance is disrupted and the traveler gets distracted, often seeking to fill their pleasure and stimulation needs in varied, sometimes subconscious and hidden ways.

Additionally, the traveler may be unaware they are seeking to be stimulated on an emotional, psychological level and substituting; calling this stimulation need something else. Often a search for higher knowledge is an out growth of our emotional needs. In this case, the traveler may be searching for a path that provides stimulation or the ability to be with other like minded persons (social need). Having defined the search in these psychological or sociological terms, the traveler may be unaware of what a path can actually provide. Here travelers are lacking essential information and confusing one thing with another.

Part of our natural development involves interacting with

the world on many levels. By working, being with others, enjoying leisure pursuits, sharing with family and worshipping, we fill many of our basic human needs. By participating in the world, helping to make it better, we get necessary attention and stimulation. The confusion sets in when we are not clear what we want and mix the need for higher knowledge with something else; making this search an extension of the need for attention, excitement or involvement in 'something important.'

Keep in mind unless a teacher is present to help you see this situation within yourself, often it will get over looked. When one speaks about being truthful in regards to the path, this is one of those areas that touches everyone and must not be dismissed by a personal rationalization, 'Oh, that may be true for others, but not me.' Ask yourself, why do you want higher knowledge? What is it you expect from the path and what can you give the path?

Try a simple exercise. As you go through your day, whether it is at work or in your home life; from time to time take a few steps back and observe your behavior and the behavior of others. Assume you are confusing one need with another. In light of this routine confusion: today at the office did you go see the boss because you wanted attention, stimulation, and wanted to feel important? Or you had something useful to discuss? Was this discussion important to you or others? Similarly, did you call your spouse because you were bored, did not have enough mental stimulation at the time, or you had something useful to discuss? Over a period of time, you will be surprised how much of human behavior is centered on our basic attention and stimulation needs, and can be explained this way.

Remember this does not make our behavior good or bad. Within the context of higher studies, basic emotional needs are regularly confused with higher ones. Most people get offended when you try to point this out, so, work on yourself. In order to reach higher, each person must recognize this basic confusion within themselves.

Understanding your real motives and when you are operating at an emotional level is an important beginning. Because to advance, first you must be able to see what is really going on right in front of you; not what you think or believe is present.

ᛒᏯ   ᛒᏯ

Four fishermen approached Vesudeva and Emil. Emil noticed they were sweaty, excited and wore a sad look of concern. As they drew closer, Vesudeva graciously offered, "Please have a seat while I brew you some tea."

The lead fisherman who was the oldest in appearance, with a white beard replied, "Right now, I regret that we do not have time for that. Perhaps, another time. Sadly, we are here to inform you, that your co-worker was lost in the river. Also your raft, what is left of it we have tied to the dock. It will need many repairs."

Vesudeva stood, hesitated picking his words, then spoke, "Please, tell us what has happened." As everyone took a seat around the table, the lead fisherman replied, "Greetings. I am Wasu. These are my three brothers, Retok, Barik and Sermu. We have been hired by the local authorities to hunt and kill a rogue, river crocodile. This croc has grown unusually large, dangerous and learned to capsize boats. For weeks, this croc was tracked further north and has gradually moved south down the river."

"About an hour ago, we spotted the ferryman's raft with its distinctive platform design. Realizing the raft was captained by a younger man, momentarily this confused us. In that short delay, we believe the crock attacked. One instant your co-worker was on the raft, the next we heard a terrible roaring sound and loud cries for help. By the time we reached your raft, it was overturned and your co-worker was gone. From the attack, the waters churned with multi-colored spices that we assumed were part of the cargo. Sadly the spices and their colors combined with a deep, blood red which for yards tainted the surface."

৯০

Somewhere in another dimension, the ferryman was seated in a classic lotus position with legs crossed. His eyes were closed and sat motionless. In turn and individually, he was reflecting the Light across his heart to all his students. Seated beside the ferryman were three other faceless companions of shimmering white luminescence. All were arranged in a circle and they too took the Light from the ether reflected it across their hearts out into the world of forms. Taking turns, these beings of primal energy, projected the Light into all the dark corners of the planet.

Like the sunlight, this Light was a nutrient, a life giving and enabling factor, without which there would be only darkness. Now, each of the companions continued to reflect the Light and became absorbed totally into an orb of brilliance. Like a dynamo, their vibrations ebbed and flowed, generating and liberating this energy. Losing all individuality they were consumed and absorbed into their daily task. Giving life to the world.

৯০

Emil was distraught. His friend, Nestor was gone. How could that be? Spiritually, weren't students protected by their teacher?

Outraged Emil cried out. "How can this happen? Why weren't those who work and live along the river notified? I cannot believe this."

Softly Wasu answered, "The authorities did not want to create a general panic, trying to keep this matter quiet. For many weeks, we hunted further north. It is only over the last two days that the croc traveled south. Mainly, the croc has been feeding off of live stock watering themselves in the shallows. However,

93

we know of two other attacks. Today when we lost two men and another, where a canoe was overturned and a father and son were lost. We believe it was this beast."

At this point, Vesudeva inquired, "Can you take me out on the river? I want to see for myself and search for Nestor."

Wasu answered, "Of course. We can take you out in our boat. Your raft will need much work. In the hope your co-worker, Nestor has survived, two of our boats are currently searching. Now, we will have to notify the river people the giant croc is here. In time, we will kill the beast or he will move on. This one is rogue and cannot sit still for very long."

"Come we must hurry. We will wait for you in our boats."

ဢ

As the ferryman and Emil walked toward the dock, angrily Emil questioned, "How? I thought all of your students were under your protection. Why?"

Gently Vesudeva spoke, "Will you join in the search for Nestor? There is little that you can do here. If the croc attacks we will need another set of hands?"

"But you're not answering my question . . . Yes. I want to destroy that beast. Again, how did this happen?" Walking briskly toward the dock, Vesudeva replied, "No person is promised another day. Each moment is a precious treasure and we need to live each moment completely."

Softly Emil muttered, as Vesudeva continued speaking, "Always with the fine words and sentiments. At this moment these words do me little."

Hearing and choosing to ignore Emil's bitter reply, understanding in time anger turns to something else, Vesudeva continued, "Remember. In this matter much is hidden. As the Source Wills, the meaning of these events will be known."

Retreating inward, not caring to respond further Emil thought, "I am not much longer for this place. If Nestor is either dead or missing, come morning I will be gone. Perhaps later, the fishermen will drop me off on the far shore. Surely, the ferry will take some time to repair and I cannot count on it for transport."

∞

In that place where time stands still and the Divine enters into the world of forms, the ferryman along with his companions continued to reflect the Light across the creation.

In this world, while the ferryman searched for his missing student along the river Velo, another aspect joined in the spiritual work of the spheres. Many travelers are unaware, through higher capacity it is possible to be in more than one place at a time.

The wise claim, we are all multi-level and simultaneously exist on different planes of reality. It was in that other place that Vesudeva joined with his missing student, Nestor and assisted him along the journey.

∞ ∞

Traveler: One of the wise has said, 'the only requirement for the traveler is that the traveler desires Truth above excitement and makes his way to the teacher.' What is the meaning of this statement and how does it apply to a search for higher consciousness?

Master: Our everyday awareness thrives on excitement. Excitement is a main source of stimulation and if no real excitement exists we will manufacture our own. Daily we require multiple forms of stimulation; and much physical and mental activity is directed toward filling our basic excitement need.

For purposes of our discussion, excitement and stimulation come in two forms, positive and negative. Positive excitement is a stimulus which is perceived as a benefit, for example, "I just received a sum of money." Similarly, negative excitement might be, "I just lost a sum of money."

Both forms of excitement and stimulation are part of living and at times can be a hindrance to the traveler's movement along the path. Excitement creates a 'loud' vibration that over rides the more subtle vibration of inner awareness. If the traveler seeks excitement on his way to Truth, he will never get past this stage of worldly need; being unable to hear the faint whispers of higher knowledge; seeking a teaching or teacher that is personally exciting as opposed to a teaching that works.

The teacher exists to help the traveler maximize their higher potential; pointing out this basic discord to the traveler. The degree to which the traveler is successful, is related to the degree to which the traveler seeks Truth over excitement and follows the guidance of their teacher.

൩

Some people create problems for themselves,
So they will have something to do.
These problems are a stimulant:
To help fill an otherwise empty existence.

O traveler when will you learn:
Fill your hours with purposeful activity?

൩

— 15 —

Choice & Love

According to traditional accounts, man has 'free will' and is different than the Angels: who must serve the Source. Traditionally, Angels worship and serve because that is their nature; except for Iblis the fallen One who refused to bow down to Adam. While man may choose to worship the Light; man/women often choose all kinds of terrestrial things to worship (money, power, and self importance).

From the viewpoint of progress along the path, it is the traveler's goal to quiet personal desire and will, so that the Divine or higher capacity might manifest. In order to arrive at this inner state, the traveler suspends desire, turns inward toward the Light and the higher aspect comes forward; while the worldly self is still or transparent. When that which is tied to the world is absorbed in Divine love; as necessary that which is highest presents and acts.

Daily the traveler chooses to submit to that which is Highest. This is the Divine Plan and plays out each moment of our life. In every thought or action, we must consciously choose to reach higher or stay where we are. Many of the exercises, prayers, teaching discussions and context of the learning situation focus upon how to do this. Within each, there is a spark that is of the same fabric as the Light. Through the teacher's direction, the traveler learns to recognize this aspect and daily turn inward toward the Light. This is the primal prayer and orientation. The journey is to do this while participating in the world and to consciously serve the Light, every moment of the day.

For most people, one of the challenges of daily life is to select those things and experiences which are beneficial or good. This good may be personal, societal or related to that which is higher. Often this is done based upon belief or appearance of goodness.

At a certain point, the spiritual traveler knows what is in accord with the higher. For someone who has reached this level, it is not a matter of believing or feeling something is good or bad. There is an inner capacity that knows what to do. Words like good or bad are secondary and have no practical meaning. Action is based upon knowledge that flows from the Source. This capacity to know may be permanent or come and go based upon the necessity of the situation. The completed traveler has an inner capacity to choose that which is necessary. This capacity is inborn and over a period of training is refined.

In life, one of the most challenging things a person learns is to have their needs and desires become secondary. Doing something for someone else and not feeling resentful is a difficult lesson. Yet when someone loves, it is easier to give without emotional attachment. Consider the love a mother offers her crying newborn. Is the baby caressed because the mother expects future consideration? Does the mother freely offer a kiss or worry about not being able to watch her favorite television show? The magical element, which places the focus away from self to something higher, is love.

Pray because you love the Light. Seek to make your life an hour of service; because you are a lover and burn to be with your beloved. In time, that which is higher will manifest; you will fulfill your destiny as representative of the King and in each thought and action rich higher.

₭   ₭

Vesudeva rode in one boat and Emil in another. As these craft were built for speed and maneuverability, there was limited passenger space. Each boat was shaped like a cylinder, eight feet long, containing two fishermen. One fore and one aft. In the rear, the stern man paddled and steered the craft, while the crewman in the bow paddled and scanned the river. Along with supplies, passengers were seated mid-ship. Quickly, these two craft pushed off and headed out into the river to join their sister boats searching for Nestor and the croc.

Emil sat in the middle of the second craft. His mind was racing with multiple thoughts and fears. He was angry and when he gazed up ahead he saw the back of Vesudeva's head and grew angrier. Then Emil realized, he had expected Vesudeva to protect Nestor and Vesudeva failed badly. Vesudeva was sitting very still, with head bowed and Emil began to wonder. Can Vesudeva read my thoughts and know what I am thinking?

As Emil's mind raced, his heart beat faster and faster. All he wanted to do was get away. He wanted the fishermen to drop him off on the far shore, right now, so he could run back to his old, safe life.

The thought of searching for a monstrous, killer crocodile and his best friend's body, scared him deeply. Emil no longer cared about the article he was writing. Now the article seemed irrelevant and unnecessary. Besides, why write it? What kind of holy man cannot protect his students? Also, if Vesudeva could not protect Nestor, certainly he could not protect himself, Emil or the other fishermen.

Continuing to shake, Emil told himself that when he accepted this assignment he did not signup to become a bounty hunter for a rogue crocodile and wanted no part of this work.

₭

As the two boats that carried Vesudeva and Emil joined the others that were searching mid-river, nervously, Emil scanned the river. Here the water was deep green, indicating quick movement and extensive depth. Floating around the boats was a rainbow of spicy colors that settled on the water's surface. There were black, yellow, and chunks of white, green and light red color, now floating and mixing with the current. Emil knew that the loss of these spices had cost someone dearly and when he saw traces of a dark, blood red amidst the coloring, he realized he had lost something more precious than fine seasonings.

Emil trembled. It was a warm day but as he considered his own vulnerability he grew colder and trembled uncontrollably. What would happen if the rogue crock returned for something else to eat? Quickly he searched for a weapon and he uncovered an extra rifle, two spears and fish netting. Was this enough to protect them from that ferocious beast?

♋

By this time Vesudeva was getting a report from the sternman of one of the other boats that continued to search. "So far we have not seen any indication that your friend survived the attack. Briefly, there was a great deal of blood mixed in with the spices. This was not a good sign. As time passed there was less and less. A faint trace remains. We have been circling this area and gliding along with the current. Hoping that if he survived and somehow pulled himself to the surface. He would be traveling at the same speed as the water."

"At this point, we consider it unlikely that he made it, but were waiting for you before making a decision about moving the search. Sometimes, crocs take their food below the surface and store the carcass under a log or in a submerged cave along the river's edge. Holy one, have you any suggestions?"

Vesudeva replied, "I think we should split up with one boat remaining mid-stream in case there is any sign of Nestor and the others search the shorelines. It is unlikely that the croc traveled as far as our dock. Certainly we have seen nothing as we paddled out here. One boat should search the eastern shoreline, while the other two focus on the far western side. What do you say to that plan?"

The head fisherman, who was in Vesudeva's boat serving as sternman, nodded his consent and the search party split into three sections. Vesudeva's and Emil's boats broke from the formation and started toward the western shore while one stayed mid-stream, and the fourth paddled toward the eastern shore, just below Vesudeva's dock and hut.

ഇ

As their craft approached the shoreline, Emil was working up nerve to force the fishermen to drop him off. He did not have the stomach for the hunt and wanted to get out of there as quickly as possible. The idea of being a journalist who would debunk a religious fraud no longer appealed to him. Also, Emil longed for the warm safety of the tavern fire and the sweet taste of tavern women. Oh, how he was going to miss his old buddy, Nestor.

ഇ

In line, the two boats eased their way across the water, toward the western shore. Vesudeva's boat took the lead, followed by Emil's. Surprisingly, Emil found himself silently praying for his own safety. Emil had not prayed in many years, since he was a boy of seven. That was the winter when his mother died. Emil stayed up all night by her bedside praying that the fever pass and her life be saved. Tragically, his mother did not survive the night. Since then, Emil had not prayed for anyone or anything. He reasoned it was useless. Emil found it strange that he should think about his mother, now.

Suddenly, there was a loud RRROOOAAARRR and water began splashing all around the lead boat, up ahead. Then the boat and its three passengers were thrown five feet, straight-up out of the water and came crashing back down, atop a dark black creature of enormous shape and size. In that confusion of noise, water, breaking wood and screams from the fishermen for help, Emil realized what was happening. The croc had come up beneath the lead boat and thrown every one out. As Emil watched in terror, the fishermen in his boat jumped to action, firing their rifles to kill the beast. Emil wondered what if the croc is only wounded, then becomes angry and attacks us?

Before he was aware of what he was doing, Emil stood and dove out of the boat into the water. Taking a shallow dive away from the attack, quickly Emil pulled himself to the sur-face and started swimming, frantically toward the shoreline. At this point, safety was less than 100 feet away.

As Emil swam for his life, he was unaware his hurried mo-tion and quick dive overturned and swamped their boat. Now, both fishermen were in the water with Vesudeva and their com-panions. All were engaged in a watery frenzy of knives, desper-ation and death.

ℜ

After swimming and splashing frantically, Emil pulled himself out of the water and onto the shore. Panting and breathing heavily, Emil needed to turn quickly to see if the beast followed him. Also he wondered how the other fishermen and Vesudeva were doing. Had they somehow managed to kill the beast? Or was the croc eating someone else for lunch?

When Emil turned to assess the situation, all he could see was darkness, scores of sharp teeth and the great expansive jaws of the croc open and clamp down around his head and upper body. In that blinding moment of pain and terror, Emil felt a sheering of muscle and tissue. In that letting go of conscious-ness, Emil heard himself call out into the darkness -"Oh no! I am being eaten!"

ॐ   ॐ

Love is the magical element. Lifting man higher than angels.
For love and giving to another sets the traveler free.
Forgoing individual need the traveler gives to his Beloved
And is made more complete by this selfless act.

ॐ

— 16 —

Learning Sequence

Each traveler is a unique being and as such has an individual learning sequence. All travelers are on the path to completion. This is the Divine Command and the mission for which each soul was created and sent out into the universe. Each soul is to travel and return more complete so they can reign in Kingship.

Before encountering a teacher, each traveler must undergo preparation. Often this involves searching within him self and the world. Looking for an answer to the burning question within: the traveler is not satisfied with what has been encountered. Still there remains a yearning, an inner emptiness which is pushing the traveler toward the Source.

Because the Teaching emanates from another dimension; it operates within a framework and structure that is different than ordinary classroom preparations. In familiar learning structures, the sequence and course of study are fixed. For example, if a student is interested in learning mathematics, they sign up for a class at the local high school or community college. There is a text, the teacher meets with the students twice weekly for 60 minutes and depending upon the complexity, specific mathematical problems and exercises are taught and learned.

In higher studies, the structure is less rigid and learning occurs simply when there is something to learn. For months, the traveler may follow specific exercises and tasks to little or no effect. Then one day, because of a coming together of factors, learning is imparted. This learning is neither cognitive or emotional. A different level of energy is involved and the student perceives something finer, more subtle and holistic.

In contrast to academic presentations, higher learning occurs in a flow more uneven, and occurs sometimes at levels that may not be consciously perceived.

Another technique used is the scatter method, whereby a number of ideas are presented in different ways: dropped, picked up again, restated and dropped again. Collectively, these call to the higher consciousness and come together at the intended time and form a deeper, more lasting impact. Over time the material is absorbed, coming together at the right time, in the right place and with the right people.

This form of learning requires a highly skilled teacher who can assess each traveler's individuality and specific learning pattern. The course is always individual and based upon the teacher's assessment and requirements of the Teaching.

ɕɔ   ɕɔ

CLAP! CLAP! "Awake!"
Loudly, Vesudeva's voice and hand clapping motions commanded Emil to awake. Suddenly, Emil opened his eyes and found himself seated at the table outside Vesudeva's hut. Beside him were Vesudeva and Nestor. Both sat quietly, waiting for Emil to regain awareness and more fully understand what had just occurred.

Emil questioned, "How? How did I get here? Where is the giant croc? Wasn't I killed?"

Softly Vesudeva replied, "Give it time. Sit quietly and go over in your mind what just took place."

Momentarily there was fear and anger in Emil's eyes as he

considered how Vesudeva bewitched him. Turning quickly, Emil stared at Nestor, wondering what part he played in this deception. Emil was growing angrier.

Softly Vesudeva offered, "No. It is not like that. This experience was given to you so you could learn something."

Vesudeva signaled to Nestor, and both stood, leaving the table so Emil could work through his thoughts.

ဢ

As Vesudeva rebuilt the wall around the fire with different sized logs, Nestor checked the raft for safety, as it lay up against the dock. Meanwhile Emil sat angrily not knowing what to make out of this experience? Had he been hypnotized or bewitched? Which one was it? Why?

One moment, Emil remembered suffering a painful, coward's death in the jaws of a giant croc. The next, he was seated beside Vesudeva as if nothing happened. How was this possible? That death experience felt as real as sitting here. Emil wondered, had he really been ripped apart by the croc? Did the fishermen finally kill the beast? The raft, from where Emil sat, looked intact and there were five baskets of spices neatly stored on the dock. The spices were never in the river?

From the table, Emil could smell their distinctive fragrances. Emil wondered which experience was real. Was he really sitting here outside Vesudeva's hut or was this another illusion?

That painful death. Quickly he checked himself for wounds from the croc's teeth. There were none. When the croc bit down and ripped his flesh to pieces, he screamed for help. In that dark moment, there had been intense fear and pain but no blood. There had been no blood. Only a mental picture of pain and fear. Yes. Fear. Fear his life was over and it had been wasted.

Emil felt a tear slowly fall from his right eye and caress his cheek. No. He was not dead. Thankfully. He was still alive.

Suddenly, the flood gates opened and tears poured from Emil's eyes and he began sobbing uncontrollably. "What has my life become?" What have I gotten myself into?"

∞

While Vesudeva stoked the fire embers, he said a silent prayer for his student, Emil. Reflecting the Light across Emil's heart, Vesudeva fully realized the multi-level and emotional impact this spiritual experience was producing. The Light was a healing and life giving nutrient.

Through living and dying an alternate life, what Emil had formerly understood as reality was shaken and turned upside down. Through guided spiritual experience, Emil tasted the fragility of life and learned how each could become painfully weak and concerned only with self.

For Emil, there would be other learning experiences. Now, it was time for healing and Nestor would help with this. As the Light Willed, later, fear, anger and confusion would give way to understanding.

∞

Nestor was unaware of the specific content and level of spiritual experience that was projected to Emil. During much of the time they had been seated at the table, Nestor was engaged in a verbal question and answer session with Vesudeva.

Expertly, Vesudeva responded to Nestor's questions concerning the Teaching and the path. Simultaneously, Nestor could feel the Light being projected through Vesudeva to Emil and himself. This energy was radiating all about them. From previous experience, Nestor understood the Teaching was multi-level and operated differently, often simultaneously, on different travelers. While part of his mind learned via question and answer, another aspect was engaged with the Light.

∞

Earlier, when Nestor returned from the mid-day ferry run, he joined Emil and Vesudeva seated at the picnic table. At first, Vesudeva answered Emil's questions for the newspaper article. Then Vesudeva instructed Emil to put his questions away and Vesudeva taught Emil how to focus inward, saying the prayer. Next Vesudeva showed Emil the Light . . .

After a time of focusing inward, Vesudeva opened his eyes. Emil sat quietly, eyes closed repeating the prayer of submission and being caressed with a Spiritual Kiss. Vesudeva nodded to Nestor to ask questions. This exchange kept them occupied: until Vesudeva commanded Emil. Awake!

ॐ

It was later in the day. Nestor was waiting on his straw mat and smiled as Emil entered their hut. Excitedly Nestor inquired, "So tell me what happened. What was it like for you?"

Emil replied, "I'm not sure. I can't fully understand it all. I believe it will take me some time to understand what happened."

"Vesudeva told me just after he commanded you to Awake, that you had been given a present. Many of your questions had to be answered with a "shock.""

"Yes. I was startled and I'm still angry about what happened to me in that 'dream.' However that is not the strange part. Attached to that 'dream,' there was some kind of energy that has stayed with me, around me and traveled through me. I'm pulsating with this energy. I feel happy, safe, and fully alive, while also feeling angry and distrustful. That man has bewitched me."

Nestor laughed and replied, "Vesudeva has not bewitched you. He has shown you another part of yourself. He has awakened it. You are feeling the Light within your own consciousness. When first I was shown this part of myself, this experience lasted for 24 hours. It is a state that comes and goes."

"Nestor what are you talking about? Speak plainly."

"A state is an experience that lasts for a brief time. It comes and goes. A spiritual state shows you what is possible. It helps you define the nature of the journey. Prior to this, experience was physical, emotional or mental. Now that you know there is something else it helps define what you are seeking to learn about."

~ ~

Each traveler is a one of a kind, original, expression of the Source.
There never has been
Nor will there ever be someone exactly like you.
You are a multi-level being
Traveling through the worlds
Expressing who you are.

O traveler, learn about your self.
In this activity there is greatness.

~

Why do travelers have so much trouble accepting
They came into this world to grow closer to the Source.

While our activity in this world serves a multitude of purposes;
In some respect it will have been wasted
Unless we come to accept this unifying principle.

~

Beyond words and desires there is an underlying Reality
That unifies all things? This Reality and the method to perceive it
Is the birthright of humanity.
In their journey through this world,
Most travelers become distracted and fixate on all manner of things.
In a sense these things become their reality
And then have no need of anything higher.

~

109

That which is formless
Takes on a physical shape,
So we may know it.

৯০

Brief is our stay in this world.
Yet as we disconnect
From our higher nature,
These hours seem like an eternity.

৯০

You Are the Door

On the inner journey, each traveler is both the question and the answer. Within each there is a burning emptiness. This discomfort and friction pushes the traveler onward to find the missing piece. Searching occurs on multiple levels.

One of the great mystics described this process of burning: as a fire that has started deep within a log. Here the wood is moist and takes time for the fire to consume all the residual moisture. First there is smoke and low amounts of heat. Then in time, this low level of heat and burning dries out the log; and the fire pushes outward more strongly to consume the wood. Also, the fire is burning on the outside as well: with heat and flames working their way inward. In time, both sources of heat meet and the wood is aflame; entirely consumed by the inner and outer burning.

Another way to describe the journey is that you are the door that stands in your own way. Learning or awareness occurs through a process of removal of layers as opposed to adding information. Deep within resides the answer or higher consciousness. This consciousness has been blocked by years of selfish thoughts, specific ideas and daily requirements of living in the world. The mystic's journey is to learn to push this door aside, or quiet these thoughts so something else might come forward. Meanwhile, this consciousness or inner spark has been ignited by contact with the Teaching and is struggling to break free and come forward. That which is hidden strains to manifest, and awakens depending upon the requirements of the situation. Momentarily pushing outward, until the contact is more firmly grounded. Then the traveler turns inward, by pushing aside the door.

Remember, our worldly consciousness is needed to live in the world and participate in every day life. Even in the most highly attuned, the higher consciousness comes and goes depending upon the requirements of the situation.

A third way to describe the journey is to imagine that your heart or inner awareness is a mirror that has been clouded over by thoughts, ideas and years of selfishness. The mystic's journey is to wipe this mirror clean so that it can more aptly reflect the Light. The Light originates in another realm and enters this realm as an enabling or enriching element. In part, the role of traveler is to reflect this Light into the physical realm thereby illuminating the darkness. This is done daily, and the traveler must ever be on guard: to keep their mirror clean. Through living in the world, thoughts and ideas arise that cloud the surface. The traveler wipes his own heart "mirror" clean, through specific prayers and exercises.

ھ   ھ

It was early evening. The sun had set and the last ferry run of the day was complete. The various travelers, merchants and families had been helped along their way. In addition to passage across the river, some were provided with directions, others with soup to fill their belly and some after hearing their story kind words of encouragement.

After finishing the evening meal, Vesudeva and his two students rested and shared the teaching around the outdoor fire.

Gently Vesudeva began, "let us close our eyes and focus inward. Now imagine yourself outside of your body. There is another you suspended just above yourself. On the self that is suspended outside imagine the Holy Name written, one letter at a time, first across your forehead and then your heart. Take your finger, from the self seated here and write the Name in shinning golden letters, one letter at a time. Feel the Light and energy emanate through each letter as you inscribe it with your finger. Concentrate. In each location, after the Name has been written, feel the Light and its energy emanate from the Name both on your heart and forehead. Concentrate on the Name and its energy. Feel its loving peaceful caress. Focus. Now stay in this place. Slowly and silently repeating the Name."

After a time of silence, Vesudeva continued. "Now, imagine your heart is a mirror. Next, imagine the Light reflecting from my heart to yours. It is coming from me. It is being gathered seemingly from the air about me. Yet it has been directed and reflected from a higher source. I am part of this chain, taking the Light and reflecting it across my heart to yours. As the Light caresses your heart and illuminates it, take this Light and reflect it out across the creation to those whom you love and perceive require assistance."

And the three travelers, sat in this position reflecting the Light. For how long, who can say? For in this activity there is no time or space only the Beloved.

ಇ

Gradually each traveler returned from the world of spirit, back into the world of forms. Gently each opened their eyes. Without speaking, both Nestor and Emil turned toward Vesudeva awaiting instruction on how to continue.

Vesudeva began to speak. "In each journey, there comes a time when the traveler realizes the goal of his long seeking. Faith and belief are replaced by direct experience and knowledge. In that moment of clarity, the spark of knowledge is rekindled in the heart by the Source itself. Like calls to like and through a gentle caress of love, the heart is set aglow with the Light of creation."

"After this initial caress the process is of realization through the Light and practice. Gradually the traveler is taught through the teacher's direction, how to reflect the Light on their own. Clouding over the mirror of the heart are years of selfish living, misunderstood truths and distractions. This 'dust' or 'film' must be wiped clean, pushed aside for a time, so the mirror is clear and can reflect the Higher into the physical world."

"Within each consciousness are many streams, yet these streams are not the river. To arrive at the river, the stream must be traveled. Gradually the traveler learns to identify and go beyond them."

"Another way of saying this is that each has within ideas and thoughts that are necessary for worldly life. In order to perceive what is beyond the physical, these must be stilled for a time."

"Remember: each traveler needs all these thoughts, ideas and yearnings to participate in the world. Yet in our activity these must be quieted so something else can emerge and come forward. The higher consciousness cannot operate effectively when there are inner distractions."

๛

Next Vesudeva looked at Emil and indicated, "Ask me your questions."

Emil who was still filled with doubts about the dream experience, inquired, "Vesudeva why was I made to experience one reality, the reality of the crocodile, when in fact there was another? Why this deception?"

Smiling Vesudeva gently replied, "Each traveler learns in the way that best suits them. This is a journey of individual and collective reality. This reality was presented in a way you would learn from the most. Through the Light, it was engineered by others and projected into your consciousness, so you would know what is real."

"Each traveler experiences the multiple levels of reality in varying degrees. For all it is the same reality, yet manifests individually."

"Sadly, many go through the physical world unaware of the other realm. They are closed off to this by their own beliefs and consciousness. They remain deceived by their own values and perceptions never opening to the greater reality."

"One of the lessons contained in your waking dream was that most are imprisoned by their world view, oblivious to the Higher reality which underlies everything, until they die. At the point of death, the worldly consciousness retreats. Gradually in death, they learn to see the world of spirit."

"Remember, all awaken at the point of physical death. However for a traveler who is on our path to completion, as the Source Wills they awaken in the presence of their teacher. Hence I called you from your dream like world back into the true reality- the world of spiritual learning."

E: "Why must learning be this way? In order to reach higher, why did the Source create a reality that must be transcended?"

V: "Over time you will come to answer these questions on your own. Through our system of learning you will find your own answers." "In all things we must remember the aspect of Love. Love is the energy of creation and is the single strongest manifestation of the Source. This Way of Learning was Created because the Source Loves us and wants each to rise up triumphant, as a partner in Kingship. Man's consciousness has the capacity to influence and transform the physical universe. When this is experienced we are closest to our Origin."

ଈ   ଈ

Concerning the journey, one of the great teachers has said, "Sometimes it is not a matter of adding ability, but a matter of taking something away." The traveler's misconception and other veils must be removed, so the higher consciousness may operate without interference. Part of the teacher's function is to guide the traveler in this removal.

ଈ

— 18 —

Energy Patterns

All around us there are unseen, hidden energy patterns emanating from countless sources. Scientifically, the invention of the radio with its capacity to receive unseen waves proved this to us. In everyday life, we do not see these waves or feel them, yet they exist. When you add a transmitter that sends out these invisible rays and a receiver that can catch and play them: we have evidence of these waves with music. Seemingly, these waves are all about us but without the correct device are too subtle to detect.

Additionally, the microscope has shown life forms that we cannot see with the naked eye; that inhabit the physical universe all around us. For eons, travelers have asserted that there are other dimensions that exist alongside our physical universe. These dimensions are multi-level and may be perceived when one is correctly attuned.

For the traveler, the prayer of submission acts as a tuning device to pull inward the unseen spiritual energy and slowly tune the traveler to the more subtle influences of other dimensions. The capacity to perceive this is inborn and like cable TV. Until the correct device is added, you are not able to pull in the station. Once the attunement has been made, the traveler can tune into the station whenever it is indicated.

Keep in mind that much of our consciousness and awareness has been programmed into us. This programming and suggestion starts at a very young age and we look to describe the universe in the ways we have been taught.

For example all of us have been taught that angels have wings. That there are ghosts in cemeteries and very holy people have 'halos' about them. Consider the possibility that these ideas and formulations are approximations of what actually exists. Each person is an individual receptor of energy impulses and each receiver is subject to the influence of imagination and interpretation. Perhaps these phenomena were described at one point and they changed. Or this is one type of expression and there are multiple expressions. Be cautious and do not let your need for classification and order override your own capacity to perceive what is actually present. The spiritual dimension has many levels with countless manifestations. To see what is actually present and not what you believe is present, is the sign of advanced development.

Every person has spiritual capacity. It is one of the characteristics of 'world sickness' to deny this; holding fast to the reality of this physical time and place. Because we limit our own capacity to see and use this dimension, we are bound to certain limitations which restrict our understanding; causing many of the problems around us.

ஐ   ஐ

It was midnight and the moon was shining its light across the Velo River Valley. On the river bank, Vesudeva was seated in a meditative position, watching and listening to the river as it journeyed to the sea. In the water, he could see the moon's reflection and his own. Gradually, he focused his eyes upon the twin reflection and became one with it. And as he focused with deeper concentration, turning further inward, his higher soul began to sing.

"We are all travelers through the dark night and must remember the sun's light continues to shine even in the evening. The sunlight across the moon is reflected to the river valley and water. In turn each traveler is like a moon to a larger sun, receiving light and sustenance from a greater source. The teacher reflects the heavenly rays to the student, who in turn reflects the Light to others."

"All about this wonderful universe there is motion and energy patterns that contribute to an inter play of factors. We are the ones who forget that the universe and its many stars are evolving, and transforming themselves into something else."

"Each traveler is a complex interplay of energy, motion, activity and latent potential. Each seeks to become something greater. Fashioned from a design that is waiting to be completed. Each traveler is unique and born with the capacity to become something more -to join in the handiwork of reaching higher, and fulfilling individual potential."

෨   ෨

Both Nestor and Emil were not sleepy. As they lay on their straw mats, Emil called to his friend, "What do you think Vesudeva does when he sits and travels inward?"

"I have questioned Vesudeva about this and he has told me two things. First, the answer to this question is not really related to my journey. I should seek to answer this question for myself. Second, during this time he seeks to align himself with the Higher Factor or Source. In part, his work in this realm is to help others reach their full inner potential. In his time of contemplation and prayer: he does many things. What he did share were two aspects that relate to my journey. First he monitors and spiritually assists others who are assigned to him. Second he listens and moves to his own soul which has its own agenda and movement."

"H'mm. That's interesting. What do you think Vesudeva meant by movements of the soul?"

"According to our teachings, each traveler exists simultaneously on multiple planes of existence. Each of these planes is filled with energy that supports and directs this existence. One model, describes these planes as the physical, mental, and noetic plane. In each of these planes, there is another aspect or consciousness which joins within the framework of the soul to support and direct existence. We are multi-level, with degrees of conscious energy that can be directed for many uses across different planes of reality."

"How does this highly esoteric discussion relate to my basic question about Vesudeva's soul?"

"Vesudeva has told me that he is master of these energy patterns and levels of reality. By learning to recognize these energy patterns within himself, he has learned to see these in others and help set their higher potential free. This is the higher, creative and enabling essence within us all. This higher essence is most like the Source itself and at its deepest level acts in accord with the Divine Creative Potential. Each is a traveler of many journeys. Within each journey we learn to reach higher until we grasp our full potential -joining the Source in Kingship."

"This is a very cumbersome philosophy. I am confused how it applies to every day life? Can you make this simpler?"

"From what I understand, within each moment, there is higher potential. Most people call this higher potential doing my best or doing well for others. Yet, often it is difficult to know the best outcome of specific events or know what the best potential might be. To further complicate this, often potential outcomes lead to other outcomes. This is the ripple effect."

"I'm having trouble with this."

"Let me give an example. When you come upon a beggar

in the street and this fellow implores a donation or alms in the Name of the Source, how do you know to give or not?"

"Well there are rules of our faith that govern this situation. For example, it is better to give than receive."

"This is true, but these are general rules and the question arises, does the general apply to the specific? Let us assume you have only a small amount and you need it to pick up food on the way home for your family. Do you give to this fellow who may spend it on drink or drugs or do you use the funds for your family?"

"I'm not sure. I guess there are further rules that apply to this as well."

"There are. However, once again how does the general rule, first care for self and family, then help others, apply here?"

"The first rule, 'better to give than receive' does not apply here, not, if I follow the second rule and care for my family?"

"Remember, each of us has an inner capacity to help discern what each situation requires. This is the higher consciousness or spiritual knowledge and it can be very specific."

"Perhaps, this inner, intuitive knowledge tells you give the poor fellow the money and your family will benefit from this act of charity. They can eat what they have and this fellow will not go without. In this kindness, there will be benefit for all."

Growing impatient with this argument, Emil replied, "I guess this will work if everyone in the family goes along?"

"What if two agree and one disagrees?"

"I don't know! I'm tired of this tedious scenario! What is your point and how does it apply to me?"

"My point in all of this is that each has for the most part latent higher capacity. After a period of preparation it is meant to be used in every day life. This capacity is designed to help people lead more complete and fuller lives. This capacity is holistic and integrating, intuitively knowing what the situation requires."

"Vesudeva is master of this capacity. Part of his role is to help others recognize and use this capacity. Because this capacity is not visible or easily quantified, most people deny its existence. This dimension has its own rules that I am just beginning to understand and accept."

"Further a body of knowledge and experts exist in this area. They are our greatest resource and hope for the future."

∞   ∞

O man you are a being of conscious energy.
Arise and accept who you are.

Why do you deny this aspect of self?
This is the factor that will set you free.

∞

When I am no longer here
I will have become a ray of Light
Traveling through the air.
I will dance and sing
Before the smiling King.

My body will be no more
And through the galaxy I will soar.
A spirit of radiant love
That will glisten on the universal seas.
Reflecting the Light for all eternity.

∞

This morning as I slept the sun caressed my lips.
Passing love and warmth in the kiss.

122

Then I awoke to brighten the day.

൰

— 19 —
How to Lead an Original Life

In any form of learning, travelers require a structure. If you wish to live an original life and fulfill your own, individual destiny, follow these principles.

- Strive to lead a balanced life and avoid excess.

- Enter into the mainstream of your community. Strive to become an 'ordinary' citizen within the society you find yourself.

- Seek to help others.

- Embrace excellence. You have many abilities.

- Say the prayer of submission each morning and evening. Prayer is intended as a joy not a burden.

- Follow the religion of your birth and fully embrace it. This is a starting point for more advanced spiritual study. If you are not able to follow the religion of your birth then say the prayer of submission or seek another Path.

- Abstain from mind altering drugs and stimulants. Rarely use alcohol.

- Follow your heart wherever it may lead you. You have a Life Plan and must learn to follow it. You do this by listening to your heart.

- Spiritual learning is part of life. It is intended as a center from which to come forward. Lead a complete life. Use all of your abilities.

- Avoid people who are obsessed. Be someone who is not "weird" and is normal. Try to be someone whom you would trust.

- Remember to trust yourself. You have everything you need inside of you; you have been given enough for the journey. Listen to your higher self -it knows your Life Plan.

- Make your way to the teacher.

- Remember, travelers are different and there are many paths. Find your own path; embrace and follow it.

An original life is a life that is lived in accord with the Higher Design, and your own individual Life Plan. The process of following your Life Plan, implies the traveler works to use their many abilities in the world and has reached a level of personal maturity.

A Life Plan is an inner 'blueprint' for the course of your life and includes those things you wish to accomplish; and identifies factors necessary for accomplishing goals. To enact your Life Plan you bring with you the skills, talents and temperament necessary to accomplish what you have come here to accomplish. Aspects of your Life Plan remain hidden until they emerge, and are enacted; this hidden dimension is the province of the Unseen Forces.

Your Life Plan does not require that you do something dramatic. It requires that you do something purposeful and become someone who is useful. The servant seeks to serve and be of use. Fulfill your potential by traveling to all the parts of yourself; remembering daily that you are the son or daughter of a King. Seek to make your life a song and prayer to the Highest; both in yourself and the universe.

ஐ   ஐ

It was morning. Vesudeva, Nestor and Emil were seated at the breakfast table. As planned, Nestor would work the ferry while Vesudeva and Emil completed their interview for the newspaper article. Emil's planned visit was drawing to an end and in order to meet the deadline he had to start writing. Also, Emil needed to clarify some points and more fully understand Vesudeva's viewpoint.

As the three travelers sat together amidst the trees that lined this quiet spot beside the river, Vesudeva held up a seed from a half eaten fruit. "Within each seed there is a potential and a plan. Combined with the natural forces of sunlight and rain and a host of other factors this seed reaches completion. It becomes a tree bearing fruit, thereby serving the purpose for its life. Then, when this form ends, moves onto another type of existence."

"In many ways man is like this seed. There is an inner potential and with the correct interplay of factors becomes a tree that feeds the countryside."

ஐ

E: "Vesudeva if you were to summarize your philosophy into one simple guideline for travelers, what would that be?"

V: "The first commandment. Love the Source with all your heart and soul. Make your life a testimony to the Source's Love and with each movement, try to be like the Source."

126

E: "This seems very simple. Yet practically, how would this work?"

V: "Love or the Light is the binding force of the universe. It is the mother and father of us all. When we love, the human spirit and potential soar toward the sun. When the lover acts, it is out of love and the action is complete."

E: "From your perspective, why is there evil in the world?"

V: "Because we were not created complete and must strive toward this completion. Evil or incomplete activity is that which distances us from our own higher nature and the Source. Good is that which unites us with our higher nature and the Source."

E: "But war and all the murder, rape and plunder. Isn't that more complicated than simply action that distances or brings us closer?"

V: "As we have discussed in war there is great variability and learning. With many opportunities to bring the traveler closer or create distance from their higher self. Sometimes wars are fought to protect family and other times to make the leader rich. Remember, any activity can be used to bring you closer to the Source and your higher destiny. Often it is a question of attitude and intent. This factor alters the energy and potential of the situation."

E: "Today many people refuse to believe and spend extended periods pleasuring their bodies with drugs, alcohol and sex. For our readers, can you comment on this activity?"

V: "First, our bodies in part were created as pleasure machines. In the correct amount and right circumstance, these things can be fun, pleasurable and are part of life. Often it is a question of attitude. Excess in anything can be destructive, bad and not in accord with your best interest. Also most people's belief system or religion specifies the circumstance under which these activities are permissible. Some people accept these conditions and others do not. From our perspective, the operative factors are attitude, circumstance and degree to which one participates in these activities."

"As to the first portion of the question, that today many people do not believe and turn toward these potentially destructive outlets for support and guidance. Remember, in everyone's journey there is a time when they doubt and do not believe. This is a natural phenomenon and necessary to a fuller and more complete development. We require people who have questioned, doubted, and then come to some agreement and acceptance. We require a mature decision as opposed to an engineered and indoctrinated belief."

E: "Your view on war, drugs and sex seems very simple. Are these activities not more complex?"

V: "People know what is right and wrong. Each person has an inner sense of what is best for themselves and others. Usually people learn these differences at an early age. Second, in all things there is both a simple and complex answer. These activities have been with the human race since the beginning and serve multiple purposes. Each must become adept at understanding their own motivation and inner need. In understanding these factors the traveler can become master of them and learn to suspend feelings and thoughts, for a time, so something else might operate and come forward."

"You see we are primarily interested in a higher outcome. In order for this to occur the traveler must be adept at pushing aside secondary phenomena."

E: "What do you say to enrolling young children in a given faith? Often well meaning parents enroll youngsters at a very early age into a specific type of religious training; these youngsters may not completely be ready to have. Later as adults these same people rebel against this childhood instruction and belief system. What should parents do?"

V: "In all learning there is something termed, degree of understanding. Some people need a basic understanding of a subject and others require advanced levels. Religious learning has many levels. Some people are content with the faith of their birth. For them it is beautiful and helps them establish a good life. Others need to rebel and find something different that better suits them.

"The religious training of one's youth for many is intended as a framework or starting point. Then as the person grows older and advances, deeper, fuller learning occurs. These are advanced students who may be within their own original faith. Then there are others who require what we offer. What we present is compatible with any of the great faiths. According to tradition, it is the heart of all religious teaching."

"In order for a religious teaching to manifest in the world, it must have both an inner and outer expression. Many times, the great faiths only provide this outer form or basic level to learning. All faiths have this inner dimension as well. However, this inner level is either dormant or difficult to access. This is for a variety of reasons and many religious teachings have focused on the external."

E: "Can you elaborate on the inner and outer form of religious teaching?"

V: "Yes."

E: Smiling. "Would you please provide us with example of an outer expression?"

V: "Many faiths have prayers, rituals and activity that have existed for many years. These are outer expressions of faith. These have become traditional. Often people engage in this activity without connecting to the inner current. Many faiths accentuate emotional expression. Their services are geared to evoking either an emotional or intellectual response. For example, "Now I understand what that concept means." Or, "I felt so at peace during that service." Or, "I felt closer to God and wanted to help based upon what that preacher said."

"The higher element manifests differently. It is beyond physical description. Feelings, moods, desires and understanding become secondary to true, inner knowledge."

"There is nothing wrong with wanting to help or feeling closer to God. From our perspective, however, these are emotional responses and something else is possible only with the correct perspective and training. Each person has this capacity and under the correct circumstance it can be brought forward."

૭૦   ૭૦

Many make religion too complicated of a thing.
Religion should be natural
And as refreshing as a clear, cool drink of water.

૭૦

While shopping, have you ever considered how many brands and varieties of water are available? There is natural, cold spring, hot spring and countless sport drinks with carbonated waters.

Also at meals, have you ever noticed how rarely water is the beverage of choice? In some restaurants you have to ask for water before they will even serve it. It is not uncommon for some children to go days without a plain glass of water.

It is the same with mankind's religion. For most, the spiritual water must be sweetened before they will drink it.

છ

— 20 —

Consciousness

In this age we are exploring the various dimensions to consciousness. Particularly how thoughts influence our health and life. For our purposes, consciousness is defined as thought, awareness and directed energy from mind. Mind being that part of the soul that is intelligent and governing. Our body and its energy are creative extensions of this awareness.

In the past, our culture has made 2 basic distinctions between consciousness (i.e., either conscious or subconscious). Yet other cultures and scientists have studied this area for millennia. Some of these travelers have defined types of consciousness that exceed hundreds of categories; now, we are beginning a further exploration and defining the limits.

From the mystical perspective, there is an aspect of man that is lasting and has multi-level awareness. For a time, this awareness has taken up residence in a physical form to learn, work and serve. The physical body affords different methods of learning and service. This awareness or consciousness is the directing and defining element for it generates its own creative potential. It is this aspect which incorporates the learning and takes it forward.

With consciousness there is energy and the potential to create, within certain limits, individual reality. This reality may be within your mind or in the larger physical world. Conscious energy through a vibration has the potential to pull things toward or repel. For example, the person who has a dream or idea and works to bring this into the physical world; is using this energy to create or bring toward them the dream they see inwardly.

Prayer is another form of conscious energy that is directed. This energy operates under a set of rules or potentials that we do not fully understand. Yet prayers, under certain circumstances, do get answered. When this energy is directed out into the physical universe it looks for a sympathetic energy pattern upon which to attach itself. When this occurs, events are reorganized and seemingly the prayer is answered.

All thought energy has a physical vibration. It is this vibration which attracts and repels. Seemingly some people are calm and others jumpy. This appearance of temperament is actually their physical vibration from their consciousness; which is directed out as energy through muscles and tissues. In part, this vibration is what others feel as calm or jumpy.

Also as thoughts are energy, this energy has a signature and may be perceived by others under certain conditions. Similarly, this energy has permanence, extending into other dimensions, which may be read by those who have this capacity.

In our time we have learned that certain thought patterns are destructive to health. For example, stressful thoughts are a factor in high blood pressure and others are more beneficial, cause a meditative state of calmness and healing. It is said, that he who can control his own thoughts for the most part can control his life and to a degree health.

� ஃ

The question and answer session continued. Emil asked the questions, while Vesudeva provided the answers.

V: "Each teacher's view of the cosmic reality is slightly different and from our perspective religious forms vary according to time, place and people. The Teaching is both transcendent and specific."

E: "Can you elaborate on this point? How can something as important as religious teaching vary? Or why does the instruction change?"

V: "The Teaching is life giving and life occurs at a specific point in time. Similarly the Teaching is perennial and timeless. From the perspective of time or creation it has always existed."

"Let us take for example a man. This man is born into a specific time and place. He is a citizen of a town and country. Also, he is a member of a family and will enter a specific trade or profession. His life will vary from others of that time. However, it will have elements that are specific to only that time and place. Consider a man who is born into a rural village, just before a revolutionary revolt by the populace and his village is ravaged by the flu virus. Clearly this external world will influence who he is and who he may become. These factors being independent of individual temperament and desire.

"According to most religious teaching, there is an aspect of man that once he dies will live on in another dimension. We term this the soul or spirit. According to tradition, this aspect is timeless.

"The Teaching is like this. It takes on a current form that is useful to the person in their present life. Additionally, on another level it is universal and transcendent."

E: "This seems to explain why some teachings emphasize one thing, while others emphasize the exact opposite. Can you further elaborate for our readers?"

V: "The Teaching can manifest in any form. The Divine is present in everything and people become confused by multiplicity. They have an expectation and desire that their way of thinking and believing must be shared with everyone. Or their way is correct and your way wrong. This is the view of the youngster. Someone who has not matured in this aspect."

"Similarly teachers will emphasize different prayers, exercises and their presentations vary. This variation is to help make the Teaching accessible to the student. While people are the same, they are also different and variation in presentation exists to help the student grasp the message."

"Typically the teacher is from the community in which the student lives. In this way, the teacher, because he lives among them, can bring forward a vibrant and useful expression of the timeless. The teaching is updated in a modern form, so, the student can learn in an accessible fashion. This is our way."

E: "What of the presentations that have not changed over thousands of years? Are these correct presentations?"

V: "One must be cautious in calling another's teaching either correct or incorrect. Does the presentation meet the traveler's need? This is our criteria."

"From our perspective, for our students, the teaching must be continually updated by a living teacher. We are about a student achieving individual excellence and full potential. According to our view, each student requires a teacher who has traveled this way themselves. This type of teacher helps assure the student will not get lost. With the teacher's assistance, the student learns and reaches completion. Then passes the learning on to others."

E: "To those readers who may not fully understand, what do you mean when you refer to The Teaching?"

V: "The Light is that perennial aspect, created by the Source to give life to the universe. The Light extends a part of the Source into the world. It enables, creates and makes all things possible. It is life giving energy that is all-wise, loving and most helpful.

"We call this energy or aspect the Light, because it dissipates darkness. When the Light is projected to a heart, the recipient learns and actualizes potential. Each traveler has this energy within, located near the human heart and that is our lasting self, providing form and direction to our lives. This aspect while similar to the Source -is not the Source. However at certain levels, has attributes of the Source."

"The Teaching, directs, creates and is the governing factor. It is primary and at the center of created being. We have no other words to describe it other than aspect, but this aspect can be perceived or experienced daily by the traveler."

"In fact, that is the journey to consciously experience this continually and use this knowledge in daily life. Man is a representative of a King having King-like attributes and abilities."

E: "For the average person, what can they expect as a result of following your Way or Teaching?"

V: "First our students follow our teaching because they must. For them there is no other Way. This way is the inner path of all the great traditions. It is the inner path to completion."

"As a result of this learning, the traveler can anticipate added responsibility and attunement to a higher destiny. Humanity is evolving to a higher condition. That is the destiny of the

136

human race. This path or Way exists in part to help enable this purposeful evolution, one traveler at a time."

"The end product of this learning is a fully developed human being who is awakened through the activation of certain, inner centers. Also this capacity has been matured through being in contact with a living Teacher, and is used along with other capacities to live a fuller life, making the world a better place. Service to humanity is the end product of learning and development."

E: "In the process of understanding self and realizing potential, what can you tell the prospective student they can expect to learn?"

V: "Man is the meeting point of both heaven and earth. He has within aspects of both worlds. Also man is representative of the Source and as such has a divine destiny throughout the worlds."

"The task or journey is for the traveler to explore all the parts of self and embrace all characteristics. The traveler must journey to all the different parts of self to know who they are. In this journey of discovery and exploration, they learn many things and become mature. They are more fully able to embrace their destiny of service."

"In this world, we are to make our lives a song of celebration; reaching out to others by living a complete, original life. Within each there is potential to bring forth a fully developed person who is an excellent, more complete version of themselves."

"When the traveler moves on to the next phase, they will have begun the work of that next phase in this world. Fundamentally, we are multilevel beings who have come to this world for a time, then journey onward."

"How you spend your life is up to you. What we offer is the perennial path to completion presented in modern form."

E: "What if the traveler has a different faith? How does your teaching relate to them?"

V: "If the traveler has found a path, tell them follow it to the end. Encourage them to be a better Christian, Jew or Muslim. Tell them to use their faith to make the world better, bringing people together, calling the Name in all its different forms."

"We are there with our Path for those who cannot travel any other Way. This is their Way."

E: "Are you saying that all the paths are true paths? If this is so then why the animosity?"

V: "To answer, let us use the example of river craft, such as a row boat, canoe or raft. Each of these craft transports the traveler across the water and performs their function satisfactorily. However, some crafts move faster, some carry more passengers and others handle better in choppy water. Depending upon the task, they have been designed differently and are expected to function according to their design. Although different, these crafts all carry travelers across the water."

"Now if one Captain begins a discussion that his craft is better than the next fellow's, this discussion might become heated, leading to a disagreement or even a physical fight. Depending upon the participant's personality and real motives, any discussion about river craft might be useful or destructive."

"Remember, people use all types of things to make points about their individual superiority. It is the same with religious teachings. Using one thing for another purpose."

"All men are brothers with similarities and differences. Readily, people speak to the differences for all kinds of selfish and personal reasons, advancing negative outcomes that lead to wars and death."

"From our perspective, all that matters is whether a teaching or faith works. That is, helps create better people who make the world a better place."

"Religious difference exists because people across history are different. However, we must not neglect to remember the similarities."

"Like the variety of river craft, each craft transports the traveler across the water."

ഇ ഇ

Religion may be compared
To a great river that feeds the land.
The river winds its way as a mighty force
And smaller tributaries are formed
To serve the distant regions.
Some are satisfied
To drink of the small stream
And forget they must travel
The river to its Source.

Beyond the river's gate,
The Ocean is waiting.

ഇ

— 21 —

Death & The Commanding Self

Throughout the traveler's journey there are 'road signs' that are indicators of increased intuitive perception. In order for the higher to manifest in the lower, the lower must bow and make way. Often this is described as death or stilling of desire so that which is hidden might come forward. According to one of the Teachers, another way to describe this state is that the ordinary consciousness becomes transparent to allow higher perception to operate. In this state, the traveler is then able to perceive another person's need and as answer, offer that which originates from a higher plane.

The physical body one day must taste death. That is part of the design. The ordinary consciousness is fearful of its own end. It is tied to the physical body and death of body is a death of consciousness and awareness. Yet that which is transcendent also resides in the same house and is able to offer under the correct conditions an answer of its own. Death is but a door to a different existence. Yes, there is bitterness about death but you must give up yourself to find yourself.

In order to still the worldly consciousness, a period of preparation is required. Often this training requires time with a teaching Master who through concentration and other exercises displays to the student what is blocking their own inner awareness.

Spiritual capacity is multi-level and manifests subtly. It must be perceived and cannot be forced. This essence operates under its own set of rules and typically will not operate if another part of the consciousness is 'alive.' That is why strong feelings for the most part are to be avoided.

It is a matter of removing something rather than adding. You must learn to remove the door that is in your way. This door is made up of assumptions, feelings and the way we look at the world. This aspect of consciousness is termed the commanding self.

This burning or love the traveler feels for the Divine and that sustains him/her is different than a desire for specific food or sexual activity. These expressions are aspects of the commanding self and the traveler is learning to go beyond this level of consciousness.

When the mother stops what she is doing to feed the young babe, she is giving up a part of herself so that something else might operate. It is the same in the spiritual realm.

ഐ   ഐ

It was evening. All through the day Emil questioned Vesudeva for the information necessary to complete the newspaper article. Now, Emil finished asking questions and was reviewing Vesudeva's responses, trying to condense the material into a 1500 word format. This written summary would be presented to the Editor, who would indicate from the material, what direction to take the larger article.

After a long day of ferrying passengers across the river, Nestor joined Vesudeva and Emil around the fire. This was their final evening together. In the morning, Nestor would travel with Emil back to the city. It was time for Nestor to return to his responsibilities in the market place. After all he was a carpet salesman. The world needed fine carpets and with

Nestor's training, he saw more clearly the importance of participating in the world.

Vesudeva sat quietly and motioned to both travelers to close their eyes, offer up the prayer and focus inward.

છ

After a time of drinking in the timeless and traveling to the deeply hidden, in turn, each traveler opened their eyes returning to the world of forms. Softly Vesudeva began to speak, "In time, what we have done here these last few days will be shared with others. That is the nature of this honey. The sweetness is made to be shared and offered to everyone. According to their own need, in time, others will interpret what we said and did. Emphasis will be placed upon one point then another. People will discuss what was meant by this action and what was meant by that phrase."

"Now while all these things are factors, they are not the real teaching. The real teaching is what the traveler experiences and perceives inwardly. While some of this energy will still be attached to this presentation, in time it will diminish. That is why it must be renewed periodically and given new life energy."

"What has been presented is a way to learn. A form of words, exercises, rules, thoughts and experiences must be presented in a structure whereby the timeless might enter and caress the soul. Yet it is the caress that is the most welcome and lingers long after the learning sessions."

"Our learning exists to make the world better. One person at a time is taught how to balance themselves through a gradual awakening of their hidden centers. Depending upon the traveler, individual experiences, exercises, and prayers are offered. This learning and education is meant to occur in the world as part of ordinary life. While we are all the same, children of a King, each is different and has a specific learning tract. In our system, time apart from the world is necessary only to learn

142

specific things. Then the traveler returns to their life to further learn and put into practice this knowledge."

"According to our teaching, one student is not better than another. Each student is different and consequently how they serve and contribute to the world will vary. On a river craft, all hands, officers and captain work together to create a safe voyage. This world is diverse. This universe is without end and what you learn in our classroom is how to make the journey using all of your capacity. One of the great masters termed this-'learning how to learn.'

"Simply we teach you how to spiritually focus inward, through disarming limiting thoughts and feelings, and recognizing your own inner capacity. On its deepest level, this capacity is always tuned to the higher destiny of the universe. We teach you to recognize this potential within self and use this capacity along with your many other skills and abilities. When you are attuned with the highest- anything is possible." Then Vesudeva signaled to Nestor and Emil to close their eyes. The next portion of the lesson would be without words and perceived through the Light. In turn, Vesudeva reflected the Light to Nestor, Emil and out across the river valley.

೫

After a time and who can say how long, Vesudeva opened his eyes, returning to the world of forms. In turn, Nestor and Emil returned to the physical, opened their eyes, turned toward Vesudeva, waiting.

Vesudeva resumed the narration. "Over the centuries, much has been said and done to complicate and distort religion. Religious teaching varies because people vary and cultures have differences. Many forget this historical, sociological factor and wish to extend a specific teaching form to all people at all times. While teachings are transcendent and exist across time, as teachings age and are extended to different groups who may be divergent, something is lost. Specific practices are prescribed to specific groups for a reason. This reason may or may not be applicable to others."

"Our religion and our path, is Love of God or Love of the Source. We hesitate using the name –God– because there are both negative and positive reactions depending upon prior experience attached to this word. For many, these reactions get in their way of learning."

"Each person's time in this realm is fixed. We are born, live, then, we die. Most have no or little control over the former and later. However what we do control, to a large degree, is how we live. It is our consciousness, the things we think about and the actions which we purposefully take, that with training, is within our control."

"Make your life a song. An original life and tune. Remember, your life is meant to be enjoyed and is unique. Journey to the many parts of self. In this journey you will uncover who you are and your relationship with a King."

ဢ   ဢ

Religion is like an old power plant which has fallen into disuse. During its time the building served to fill the countryside with Light. Now its doors are closed, the windows broken and the machinery still.

Periodically an engineer arrives to rehabilitate the structure. He has expertise to direct the workers and update the building to today's specifications. Then the engines start anew creating Light for thousands of homes.

ဢ

In each person there is an organ or inner capacity of the soul to perceive the spiritual reality. This is humanities birthright and is there to be of use. Learn to listen to the soft whispering voice. It will guide you through this world and into the next.

ဢ

— 22 —

The Treasure

Within each traveler there is a place that is hidden. It is the center from which other aspects come forward. This place is like a treasure that is guarded by demons, physical obstacles, and is a long distance away. It is likened to a treasure because there is knowledge and understanding or 'wealth' attached to it. Inside, when you are with this treasure you are connected to the Source. That sacred aspect of self and all things. You want nothing and are in the process of Being.

The obstacles that stand in your way are those thoughts, worldly responsibilities and incomplete constructs that are both associated with daily life and those which are manufactured by you.

When you enter the earth phase: you bring with you those skills, abilities and talents which are necessary to accomplish that which you set out to do. In many respects, you are a complete package that requires some refinement, stretching, growing and learning. All of the raw materials are contained within and with proper instruction you can go about your life expressing yourself in relation to who you wish to become.

In this journey, what is required is a conduit or enabling factor. The Teaching and the teachers, in part, serve this function. They are the nutrient which is added; and this precious aspect is 'miraculous,' bringing forward life where there was once emptiness and yearning. This yearning and emptiness cannot be stilled by anything else. It awaits the healing ointment of 'Divine Realization.'

And in the sunlight of the Teaching's rays- that which was waiting comes forward. It is the sunlight that illumes the darkness of worldly self and leads you from selfish longing into fulfillment of self. Hand in hand these opposites carry you forward. In this worldly existence, each having a role; for this existence is one of flesh, illuminated by the presence of Being. And in the afternoon of sunlight, the flower will blossom sharing its fragrance with the meadow. Fulfilling its dream.

So dear traveler, you wish to set out on this journey and find the treasure of which I speak? You say, "No." You say, "Yes." What matter is your answer? For you are already traveling, and will only find comfort and a safe port by climbing the mountain within.

ဢ   ဢ

It was early morning. The sun was shining and the river Velo sang its song of service and completion, journeying down to the sea. Again, Vesudeva was steering and transporting travelers on his raft across the water. Over the years, as ferryman he helped many with their journey through life. Some he carried across the river and others he guided into the water of divine knowledge. Wherever there is a journey and water to cross: there is a ferryman. This morning, among the early travelers there were two farmers with baskets full of vegetables to sell in the market. Also, there was a merchant carrying metal pots that could be used to boil the farmer's vegetables. Seated amongst these travelers were Nestor and Emil. Now it was time for these two travelers to return to their city lives. Always after a period of learning comes a period where learning is applied. For you see, what good is knowledge unless it is tested and used in the market place? As the sunlight danced across the water, a blue heron effortlessly glided through the sky and our travelers eased forward with their lives. All were joined by a hidden, protective and enabling Factor. This Factor, the Mother and Father of us all, nurtured and guided them. The Life Force, the Source has promised each, 'every step you take toward me, I will take ten steps toward you.' For you see, while our journey through life is filled with trouble and tears, also it is filled with laughter and joy. And beyond this shifting pattern, there is an underlying and unifying Reality, waiting to caress and lead us forward. And within each traveler, there is an inner capacity to recognize and join with this Reality. When this union occurs, the traveler is complete with their own inner light to guide them Home.

ಉ

And Vesudeva again snapped his fingers and called, 'Awake.'

Slowly Emil and Nestor opened their eyes and shook the haziness from their mind and awareness. Gradually the two travelers realized they had been in yet another dream- like state, a world further projected by their Teacher experiencing many things. Vesudeva spoke. "So in this moment you realize that what you have just lived is a greater dream, a creation of many life times. Take this learning experience and go further. Become that which you were created to become. Become an original being of Light to shine upon the celestial seas." And Emil and Nestor smiled, realizing they were home and had been carrying within that knowledge which they sought. This knowledge was now aglow pulsating and shinning across their heart.

ಉ   ಉ

In the journey toward completion, the allegory of a treasure hunt or a search for a hidden secret is an old one. While no real treasure may exist, in terms of jewels or gold, there is indeed something that needs to be found.

The capacity to perceive or analyze every day events in a different way is the ancient treasure. Hidden within each of us is an 'organ' or inner capacity which under the proper circumstances can perceive the real patterns which shape our lives.

This capacity becomes operational only as it is used to help others and give people what they need. Not what they think they need. That is how it works.

Service at its highest level, occurs when we are able to look at ordinary events and turn them into jewels which really benefit others.

෮

Wisdom is not fine sayings or advice based upon previous experience. Wisdom is guidance and action which is in accord with individual destiny and the Divine Plan.

෮

As the willow bends to the wind
And the leaf curls to the rain,
O Lord, I surrender myself to You.

෮

Definitions

By their nature, spiritual states, stations and experiences defy written or verbal description. They are their own proof and provide their own definition. For the reader, what is offered below is an approximation or general reference point. Much like the poet's description in a love poem. The reader is provided with an artful, general description, but alas the beautiful maiden far exceeds the poet's written description. Hopefully, you will not be content with this written form and seek your own experience and definitions.

Being: emanating with energy in Oneness with the Light. In this state, the traveler is absorbed into the Light and radiates aglow through this primal energy. At the time, the traveler may be either physically active or inactive. It is an inner state.

Baraka: is the grace that is attached to all living things. It is that magical, creative, life giving and enabling aspect to the Light. It is tradition that a teaching Master is able to teach through the grace inherent in their Path and is passed on through the succession of teachers. This grace or baraka enables learning.

Commanding Self: is that part of our personality that is tied to the physical world and is necessary for daily life. Or those thoughts and concerns about worldly events, desires, responsibilities and incomplete constructs that are associated with daily life. Typically, these constructs are manufactured by the traveler, family and society as a reaction and explanation to their environment.

Completed Person: The end product of this form of learning. A fully developed and balanced human being. A person who in addition to developing all their multi-level abilities has awakened through activation of their inner, hidden centers, latent capacity. This higher capacity is developed so it can be used in service to others. That is the goal of this training.

Accounts vary, concerning the specific number of centers. In Sufism it is said there are five lataif which are viewed as concentration points located throughout the body. Locations are said to be approximations and travelers are cautioned not to try to activate these centers on their own. This can cause serious personal harm. For a fuller discussion, the reader is referred to: *The Sufis* by Idries Shah. In our story, these centers were the spices that fell into the river.

- Mind (qalb), color yellow, location left side of the body.

- Spirit (ruh), color red, location ride side of the body.

- Consciousness (sirr), color white, location solar plexus.

- Intuition (khafi), color black, location forehead.

- Deep perception of consciousness (ikhfa), color green, location center of chest.

Consciousness: is awareness of one's own thoughts, feelings and impressions. Further, from a mystical perspective, it is energy with creative awareness and potential. This awareness is in the form of multi-level energy which vibrates and forms reality at many levels.

Mind, that governing and directing aspect, is one dimension to spiritual consciousness.

Good & Evil: It is said, the completed person has an inner capacity to determine what is required (right/wrong) in any situation. For the traveler, 'good' is that which unites the traveler with his own higher nature, the destiny of the universe and the Source. 'Evil' or incomplete activity is that which distances the traveler from their own higher nature, the destiny of the universe and the Source.

Great Yearning: is the primal emptiness, void and unease which lead the traveler to search and find what is missing – the Source. This burning is on a deep, inner level. Often until the search is correctly defined, the traveler tries unsuccessfully to fill this primal need with lesser substitutes (i.e., addictions and creating life problems).

Life Plan: is an inner 'blueprint' for the course of the traveler's life. This plan includes life goals and major events and accomplishments. Also it includes those skills, talents, and temperament necessary to accomplish the life plan. When the traveler enters this phase, the traveler brings these capacities along with them. Further according to design, parts of this plan remain mysterious and unknown. If these hidden aspects were known, they would unduly influence or interfere with the life.

The Light: is that aspect, created by the Source, to give life, shape and form to the universe. That primal and perennial aspect which extends a part of the Source into the created world. This multifaceted energy, enables, creates and makes all things possible. Some term the Light, the Logos.

Mind: is that part of the traveler's soul and spirit that is intelligent, directing and governing. The traveler's body, thoughts and emotions are creative extensions of this awareness and intelligence. There is both a Universal (Mind) and individual form to Mind.

Perception: is intuitive knowledge and sight that emerges from our collective consciousness. This awareness is both holistic and integrating.

Pole: In the hierarchy or chain of transmission, the Pole is that person or point at which the Light enters and toward which others turn for their inner, direction and guidance.

When Vesudeva closed his eyes to meditate, on an inner level, often he turned toward this point.

Sincerity: This term describes inner truthfulness, and the degree to which this truthfulness is present is dependent upon the degree to which this attribute exists in the fabric of the traveler's soul. It is inherent and latent, serving as precursor to completed development.

Spiritual: According to Webster, "breathing of air. Of the spirit or the soul as distinguished from the body or material matters. Of or consisting of spirit; not corporeal." Above, except for the definition "breathing of air" which is general, even dictionaries must define 'spiritual' by itself. Hence the confusion and generality within written material. Fortunately for the traveler there is experience and the traveler knows what they are seeking.

Soul/Spirit/Heart: (1) Like the human heart, this 'heart' is the center of the soul and is that inner aspect that is most like the Source itself. (2) The soul is our spiritual form and helps give us physical life. It has both a higher and lower dimension, governing different aspects of consciousness and physicality. (3) Spirit is that 'fabric' of which the soul is constituted. It is said, the 'heart' resides in the spirit (located near the physical heart) and the spirit is housed within the soul.

The Source/God: The Source or God is that all knowing, supra-energy, consciousness that has given form and substance to the created universe. It is the Mother and Father of us all. From a mystical point of view, the Source is greater than the physically created Universe has extended a part of itself into this dimension and what is perceived by the traveler (The Light) is but a very limited aspect, or attribute of the Source.

Spiritual Greed: Excessive concern, desire and over attachment to things of the spirit. Or obsessive focus creating an imbalance, interfering with other segments of daily life. Often this condition is veiled and 'undetected' by the individual them self.

Tajjali: Tajjali is the unveiling of a spiritual reality into the realm of personal vision. It is emitted from the Source to illume the traveler who is ready to behold it.

The Teaching: The Teaching is an aspect and multi-level dimension to the Light. For travelers is the enabling factor in their journey. In some ways, the Teaching and the Light are synonymous.

Unseen Forces: Those mysterious, hidden powers and entities that govern and direct the universe, binding and setting free, according to the overall design and Plan.

World Sickness: A term used to describe a life condition, or level of awareness, whereby a person becomes overly concerned with the things of the world. This person looses sight of the importance of the higher dimension. A person who is 'infected' may be anxious and unbalanced; preoccupied with the course of daily events and fearful of seemingly secondary concerns.

Also by Stewart Bitkoff

Journey of Light: Trilogy, Authorhouse, 2004.

A Commuter's Guide to Enlightenment, Llewellyn, 2008.

Sufism for Western Seekers, Abandoned Ladder, 2011.

To contact author go to www.stewartbitkoff.com.

www.ingramcontent.com/pod-product-compliance
Lightning Source LLC
Chambersburg PA
CBHW032000040426
42448CB00006B/431